YOUR
MESS
IS YOUR
MESSAGE

HOW GOD CAN USE YOUR
BROKENNESS TO HELP OTHERS

CHAD NORRIS

DESTINY IMAGE® PUBLISHERS, INC.
P.O. Box 310, Shippensburg, PA 17257-0310
"Promoting Inspired Lives."

This book and all other Destiny Image and Destiny Image Fiction books are available at Christian bookstores and distributors worldwide.

For more information on foreign distributors, call 717-532-3040.
Reach us on the Internet: www.destinyimage.com.

ISBN 13 TP: 978-0-7684-6378-1
ISBN 13 eBook: 978-0-7684-6379-8

For Worldwide Distribution, Printed in the U.S.A.
1 2 3 4 5 6 7 8 / 26 25 24 23 22

DEDICATION

Wendy, after 25 years of marriage, I am more thankful for you now than I've ever been. I love you deeply.

Sam, Ruthie, and Jack, your mom and I have done the best we can raising y'all. Our biggest hope has been that each of you will love God with all of your hearts. We are sincerely proud of each of you. As your dad, I could not be more thankful for my children. I love all three of you. Go change the world.

Dad, "thank you" is not enough. You are a rock to our family. Kirby gave us what we needed. Go Dawgs.

Mom, I've loved you my whole life. You are tough like your daddy was. You are also one of the funniest people I know.

Mama Jane, I'll see you when my assignment is over down here. I can't wait to hug you. Thank you for everything. Only God can be the one to show you the impact you had on Gabe, Bump, and me.

BB, you are an old soul and Wendy and I are more thankful for you as each season passes. You have no idea how much you light up our lives. We love you.

Abba, to quote Larry Fleet, "I ain't too good at prayin, but thanks for everything." You are my treasure. I am Yours throughout all eternity. Thank You for saving me from hell, myself, and only You know what else. Thank You for every single blessing in my life.

ACKNOWLEDGMENTS

Shaun Tabatt, I am enjoying the brotherhood that God is growing. Fun to see so many prophetic words come to pass. Let's stay low and finish well. He's worth it.

Susan Thompson, let's be honest, if not for you I'd be in trouble. Big time. Thank you so much for making me a better writer than I really am.

Toni Bogart, thank you for speaking truth into me. All of those conversations were very helpful and I'm sure down the road that I will thank you again. I was listening more than you think.

Hammer Team, my thanks to each of you for not judging me in my mess. Y'all are some great human beings. I'd be lost without y'all.

CONTENTS

INTRODUCTION

Over the years, I have learned that not only does God want to heal us, He also highly values using our stories of healing to bless others because He is driven by both covenant and Kingdom. In covenant we find connection and intimacy with Father, Jesus, and Holy Spirit. But it doesn't stop there. Genuine covenant relationship with the Triune God leads to Kingdom building.

God loves to bless others with our stories as a way to build His kingdom on the earth. We all have a story, and that story is our message. Recently I heard Robin Roberts, a long-standing news anchor for ESPN, ABC, and other stations tell a story about how her mom told her that her mess would be her message. That statement rang inside of me like a loud bell. I don't know what your story is, but I do know that the Father wants to engage with it, and also use it to help many others get to know Him.

C.S. Lewis once said that God shouts to us in our pain. He certainly shouted to me in mine, in the most loving voice. In the darkest night of my soul, on my kitchen floor in a fetal position in the midst of prescription drug withdrawal, I found the Father. Coming off of years of high-powered anxiety and depression medications too quickly left me a physical and emotional disaster that threatened my literal sanity. Yet, here I am 20 years later, and as I look back on my journey with God, I am left to say one thing—"God is so good."

Jesus could have chosen anyone—the best, the brightest, the most capable, yet He chose twelve humble fishermen to be His covenant kingdom builders. The stories of their often-messy lives became part of the message of the Gospel. The Apostle Paul boasted of two things—being the chief of sinners, and the least of all apostles. Paul boasted in his weaknesses and maybe we should as well. God's grace flows to the lowest places. It found me on the floor, a messy, broken person who didn't know how much I was loved by Father God.

I've been a lead pastor for a long time and I have noticed over the years how many people don't realize just how powerful their own stories are. The world needs less polished superstar orators and more normal messy people who tell their stories. Your mess is your message. When Holy Spirit said, "Chad, I don't want to waste your fetal position," I knew it was time to wrap my mind around the power of God in my mess and get out there with my story. God picked me up, cleaned me up, healed me up, and sent me out with my messy message so that you can get a glimpse of His glory through my mess. He wants do the same with you. God wants your mess to become your message.

Open your heart to Him as you read this book. Take a chance on being vulnerable with the God who already knows everything about you anyway. You may discover yourself finding an authentic connection with God on a level you've never experienced. God is not afraid of our messes so why should we be?

Father, help us...

CHAPTER ONE

THE FATHER

It has been many years since I received the baptism of the Holy Spirit. I have seen things straight out of the book of Acts—healings, miracles, signs, and wonders. Yet here I am now years into walking in the Kingdom admitting that the only thing that truly matters to me is deep friendship with Father, Jesus, and Holy Spirit. This realization came into sharp focus for me after the death of a dear friend. It jarred me in a good way even though his passing took me by surprise. Having a good friend who is now standing in the presence of the God he so loves made my journey of faith so much more real. I was reminded afresh that our time here on earth is short. My friend's death put a new urgency inside of me to deeply hunger for the Father. I left the funeral by myself and became quite emotional. From the bottom of my gut I cried out, "Father, I just want to know you. I want deep friendship with you." In the weeks that followed, I began to ask myself some serious questions; to think deeply about what really matters in life. Since then, I have found that I have a clarity of thought that is bringing into focus why I am on this earth. The Father's heart is showing me that I am here to build deep friendship with Him, and to bring as many others as possible into deep relationship with Him. That what's family looks like in the Kingdom.

The Christian life isn't just about shooting up into the sky when you die. At its heart, the Christian life is about family. This idea may require a paradigm shift in your thinking. Here's an example of what I mean. I asked 25 people the question, "Who is Adam?" and 24 answered the question the exact same way. Before you read any further, think about your own answer. Once you have it, go to Luke 3:37-38. Although these may seem like odd verses to read right now, just stay with me.

> *The son of Methuselah, the son of Enoch, the son of Jared, the son of Mahalalel, the son of Kenan, the son of Enosh, the son of Seth, the son of Adam, the son of God* (Luke 3:37-38).

Of the people I asked, 24 said that Adam was the first man ever created. Only one person said he was the first *son*. "Son" is the operative word here. Why the big deal over one word? Because that one word can lead to a life-changing breakthrough of understanding, or to a serious misconception. Misconceptions are dangerous. Wars are fought over misconceptions. A misconception can lead to death, even literally. The men who flew the planes into the Twin Towers fully believed they were doing the right thing. If you believe in the core of your being that junk food is healthy for you and no one can speak truth into your life, then you may suffer a fate similar to the guy in *Super Size Me* who ate McDonald's three times a day for 30 days and almost died. Just because you are passionate about something doesn't mean you are right about it. Passion can be so overrated. A misdirected passion can become a misconception, and misconceptions can lead to death. Hosea 4:6 says, "my people are destroyed from lack of knowledge." Jesus never said truth would set anyone free. He said *knowing* the truth would set us free. (See John 8:32.) There's nothing wrong with saying that Adam was the first man ever created—it's actually a correct statement. However, the difference between the word "man," and the word "son" is like night and day. Satan likes to misdirect our understanding just a little bit so that we become more passionate about a doctrine than the reality of a Person.

In my opinion, as many as 95 percent of evangelicals in the West probably view God as a doctrine to believe rather than the One to build a relationship with. It has been my experience that very few Christians truly believe that we are literal sons and daughters of God. Granted, it's not the easiest concept to wrap our natural mind around; we need Holy Spirit inspiration for this. You see, when God created Adam, He didn't make a man, He made a son. This difference is not insignificant. We know that Adam is not the ontological son of God like Jesus Christ is, yet Paul compares the two in Romans 5 and 1 Corinthians 15. Adam came from God and bore His image. He is not just another human. He literally *came from God Almighty*. From the Scriptures, we see that God has always desired deep friendship with people. He created Adam to do more than just work in a garden. God created Adam for intimacy. They walked together in the Garden in the cool of the evening, in relationship. In Exodus 4:22, Hosea 11:1, and Jeremiah 31:9, Israel is also referred to as God's son. Even though God designated

Israel to be His chosen people for all time, like Adam, they too broke covenant with Him. Being chosen by God doesn't guarantee obedience. Obedience flows out of relationship. It's about being sons and daughters; about being family.

God desired to restore broken relationship with us so much that He sent His Son Jesus Christ to redeem the curse that started when Adam committed treason. The fruit of redemption is our deep friendship with God. That's where it began and where it ends. Jesus Christ, the Son of God, lived a sinless and perfect life and then gave up His life to be resurrected so that we too might live. He conquered the death brought about by broken covenant relationship. Jesus came to reconnect us to our Father, to get us back to Eden, to invite us to the family feasting Table. He didn't pray, "Our Father, who art in heaven, hallowed be thy name. Thy kingdom go up there. And let me take all these pathetic sinners with me and just hang on until then. God, get us there. Amen." Jesus didn't pray that way, but that is how many Christians live. Jesus prayed for our Father's will to be done *on earth as it is in heaven*. He did everything He did because He had such intimate connection, such deep friendship, with the Father.

Do you realize that the Father wants to be intimately connected and have a deep friendship with you, as He did with Jesus? I'm here to tell you that when you realize this truth, and live from this place of intimacy and friendship, it's going to change the way you see things. You will start to see through different lenses, a different set of glasses. These new lenses don't make you better than anyone else. They just enable you to see as your heavenly Father sees. God is calling you into the greatest friendship the world has ever known. He's willing to give you the time it takes to build a friendship, to learn to trust.

Because of Jesus, we are now reconnected to the Father for the closest relationship possible through the blood sacrifice of our Lord for all who confess faith in Him. When we understand God's nature, it is easier to know how He will behave toward us. God is not a doctrine to figure out, He's an actual person who wants to walk with you. This is why Jesus said "our Father" so often. The second word of the Lord's prayer is "Father."

When I first actually comprehended the first two words of the Lord's prayer, I went from being in a fetal position dealing with intense anxiety at age 28 to seeing blind eyes open at age 29. What happened? I started to believe that God is *literally* my Father. This is why the first two words of the Lord's prayer, "Our Father," are so incredibly important. The revelation in those two words changed my life. Colossians 1:21-22 says I am as clean as Jesus and presented before the same Father as holy. I'll never forget riding down the road and asking the Father, "You're telling me You love me as much as You love Jesus?" When I heard Him reply, "Yes," something happened to me in that moment. I got hungry and I started "eating." The hungrier I got, the more I ate. I discovered that the more you eat of His flesh and drink of His blood—the more you spiritually feast on Jesus, the manna from heaven—the easier it is to walk a life of faith. His yoke is easy and His burden is light. Once this revelation took hold in me, I actually started using the word *happy* in relation to spiritual things.

At the time Jesus taught the disciples to pray this prayer, they were struggling to figure out how He was doing signs and wonders. If we paraphrase Matthew 6:9-13 just a little, you can imagine the disciples saying, "Jesus, we've been watching you for a year. You're walking on water, blind eyes are opening and then there's the whole Lazarus thing; you're raising people from the dead! We know you pray a lot so how about you teach us how to pray like you." This little exchange between the disciples and Jesus gave us the Lord's prayer. Notice that Jesus didn't begin the Lord's Prayer with "our Leader," or "our General," "our King," or "our Majesty." He began with "our Father." He didn't say, "my Father." He said "our Father" because He is the father of us all. Jesus has included us in His conversation with the Father. This must have been a difficult concept for the disciples to understand.

If you remember, in the Old Covenant, God was known as a very distant person, someone far removed and remote, who didn't always come off as a warm and fuzzy God. In Exodus for example, God says very matter-of-factly, "If you don't consecrate your animals, I'll kill them" (paraphrase of Exod. 19:12-13). When Jesus showed up and started calling God, "Abba," which is Aramaic for "Our Father," it's not a stretch to think that His followers were confused. Can't you just hear Simon Peter saying, "Jesus, can we just call a quick timeout? I've listened to stories passed down from generations and generations and God doesn't seem very relational to me." Or how about Nathaniel, who was a Jew. I can imagine him thinking, "You are not sounding very Jewish, Jesus. What do you mean 'our Father'?" And things got even crazier when Jesus ascended and Paul began teaching, *"So you are no longer a slave, but God's child; and since you are his child, God has made you also an heir"* (Gal. 4:7). I think the 21st-century Church struggles as much as the 1st-century Church did to understand that we are God's family. God is about intimacy.

THE JOURNEY TO SONSHIP

I wish I could make this more complicated, but it's not. Right now, the truth is no matter what you've been through in your past, in your Father's eyes, you are His literal child. He does not love Jesus the King of Glory more than He loves you. He doesn't love Adam and Eve more than He loves you. You are His family. It is when we are so connected to Him, seeing through His eyes, that we make the journey from spiritual orphans to spiritual sons. Adam, the first son in this big family, made a tremendous mistake. Yet the Father is so good that even before He created man, He already had a plan for Jesus to come and reconcile the whole situation. He sent His Son so that whoever believes in Him shall not perish but have eternal life. (See John 3:16.)

What is eternal life? It is deep intimate connection, deep friendship with our Father, and it starts *now*, not in the sweet by-and-by. There is something inside of every one of you reading this book that longs for your Daddy. We attempt so many things just trying to get the attention of our Dad, and we do it in the spiritual much like we do in the natural. Here's an example from my family. I was hitting golf balls with my sons one day, and every time Jack, my 8-year-old, prepared to hit the ball he would wait to see if I was looking. He always does that. Before he hits, he looks and I say, "I see you," yet he never stops saying,

"Dad, watch *this* one." Our relationship with God is no different. We can be 100 years old and still asking, "Daddy, are you proud of me?" There's something inside of us that yearns for the affirmation of our heavenly Father. Many who live as spiritual orphans were actually never loved by their earthly father. This makes the whole concept of Kingdom family harder to believe but believe it we can because it is the truth, and His truth sets us free. (See John 8:32.)

We literally have a heavenly Father who is *the* majestic Creator of everything ever created. If that's not mind-blowing enough, think on this—He makes Himself small enough to relate to you as though it's just you and Him. I don't know how He does it! The moon and stars are His footstool; He knows the whole world in detail. *All* His sons and daughters are the apple of His eye, and yet He is completely focused on you as though you are His only son or daughter. How incredible is that? And guess what? You can make the choice to let this deep friendship, this incredible sonship, dominate your life. You can wake up in the morning and embrace the truth that He loves you as much as He loves Jesus Christ; that you are protected, that there is favor on you, that not even disease can separate you from His love. The truth is that every devil in hell can come at you and it doesn't really matter because He holds you in the palm of His hand. On a daily basis, Father God invites you to the Family Table where you can feast in the presence of your enemies. Slander doesn't matter, gossip doesn't matter, your past doesn't matter when you take your place at the Table. This is too good to be true and yet it *is* true! The Greek word for *too good* is *euaggelion*, which means "gospel." The Gospel is too good to be true, yet it's still true. I don't know about you, but I want the DNA of heaven to reside in me. I want to believe it in my gut. I don't want to limit myself or God by making the decision not to see through His eyes or love with His heart. I want to live "on earth as it is in heaven," by faith.

When we step into the revelation of the intimacy that is possible between God and man, the gifts, the fruits of God's Spirit, have an opportunity to explode in our lives. I've seen this in my own life. I went from having a nervous breakdown in my late 20s to now leading conferences and workshops on helping people hear the voice of God clearly and operate in power. I know from personal experience that the breakthrough we experience can give us revelation to hear the Father in the same way Jesus was able to hear Him, and to *"...do the works I have been doing, and they will do even greater things than these..."* (John 14:12).

In the Garden of Eden, Elohim took some clay, dirt, and dust and whoosh—He breathed life into it creating man. When Adam opened his eyes, the first thing he saw was God looking at him with what had to be the most tender eyes imaginable. From that breathtaking beginning the two became friends. Scripture says that Adam and God walked together in the Garden in the cool of the day. Can you imagine what that was like! Then the goodness of God made woman out of Adam's rib so that he would have a helpmate. Together in intimacy and friendship, Adam and Eve were given authority to name the animals. They had something great. They had family. They had intimacy with God. It was this beautiful intimacy that enraged satan. This fallen angel who desired to raise his throne above the stars of God, to sit enthroned on the mount of assembly, on the utmost heights of Mount Zaphon, to ascend above the tops of the clouds and make himself like the Most High (see Isa. 14:13-14) set about to do everything he could to separate man from God. He's still at it, busy trying to steal, kill and destroy the people of God. Satan wants to take the beautiful relationship you were designed to have with God the Father and steal it from you. He wants to make you an orphan.

Spiritual orphanhood mimics orphanhood in the natural. An orphan is a child with no mom or dad, who is being raised by someone who did not bring them into this world. If we are living like spiritual orphans, we confess that Jesus Christ was on the cross and that we will go to heaven when we die but act as though we don't have a Father. We search for spiritual fathers and mothers and don't understand why we can't get our satisfaction and needs met through people. Jesus said, *"And do not call anyone on earth 'father,' for you have one Father, and he is in heaven"* (Matt. 23:9). My life changed when I went from seeing Jesus as a theology to seeing Jesus as my literal big Brother. I'm not talking metaphorically. I mean that Jesus is *literally* my big Brother.

Growing up I didn't encounter a sense of happiness or joy with God. My family went to church because it's what we were supposed to do. Thankfully all that has changed for me. Now, as a pastor, I actually enjoy Monday mornings more than I do preaching on Sunday. I love just taking a walk with God. I can go to the lake and just spend time with Him, not really saying anything; just thinking about Him. My goal isn't to find material for the next sermon, or to post on social media. I just want to be with my Father. I understand why Jesus sometimes needed a boat to get away from people. He grew up in sonship and understood that life is not about performing for other people; it is about relationship with the Father. I don't say this to dishonor our earthly parents. I love my parents. Yet I know that it's possible to get to a place where our heavenly Father is more real than our earthly father. I know this sounds a little uncomfortable. You see, in the Kingdom, your earthly father is not your dad. He's actually your brother. Sounds strange, doesn't it? What does that mean? It means that your earthly father is called to steward you and present you before your heavenly Father, who is the one who created you. God is actually your real Father. In fact, we're all siblings with one Dad. Jesus Christ is our big Brother, our High Priest and our King. He's the Bridge to the Father. Jesus described the Father this way, *"for the Father is greater than I"* (John 14:28).

We should be living in the reality of such a level of deep friendship with God that we are triggering orphans all around us with a desire to know Him. There should be such a level of sonship in you that spiritual orphans don't like it. I am not talking about arrogance. When Jesus gets in you, it's actually a very humbling thing. I didn't do anything to deserve being in God's family, but you can be sure I am going to enjoy it. I'm not going to walk around like I don't have any hope. I am going to live as a son who is intimately connected with the Father; a son who is invited to dine at the family feasting Table. I'm going to live as a son who knows that my heavenly Father loves me *and* likes me. I don't have to fall apart like a three-dollar bill. I'm actually destined to reign with Him. I am a loaded weapon in His Kingdom. This is personal for each of us. We're not to live like orphans, running faster and harder trying to get to the Father. I want to acknowledge that I have already made it to the Father. If I chase Him, it is to get stronger, not to prove something. Sons grow stronger, orphans continue to seek a place to belong. You belong, not because of you, but because God wants you. You can have intimacy and deep friendship with Him because Jesus has made it possible for you to be part of His literal family.

ABBA FATHER

I think it's important that we ask the question, "Why did Jesus come to earth?" You've probably heard the standard church answer that goes something like, "Well, brother, Jesus was sent so you can go to heaven when you die." According to that answer, it's all about heaven. For a lot of people, getting to heaven is just about staying out of hell. They aren't thinking in terms of having a relationship with Jesus in heaven. For them, Jesus is simply their escape ticket out of the fiery pit. They don't understand that the Gospel is about so much more than a ticket to heaven. First John 3:8 says that Jesus came to destroy the works of the devil. What are the works of the devil? To separate us from God. Eternal life is not about going to a place. It is about intimacy with the Father who made us. It is about having an intimate relationship with Him *right now and in heaven when we die.* Jesus didn't come just to take you to an afterlife. He came to reconnect and re-establish your relationship with Abba

Father. We can know Jesus and still live as spiritual orphans instead of sons and daughters who a part of God's family. The orphan heart isn't pretty. Just look at the biggest orphan of all time—satan.

In Colossians 3:1-2, Paul tells us to, *"set your hearts on things above, where Christ is, seated at the right hand of God. Set your minds on things above, not on earthly things."* The heavenly realm Paul speaks of trumps the earthly realm and requires something from us. We have to participate. We have to shift our thinking. Take Elisha for instance. One day Elisha was doing whatever he was doing. I picture him combing his beard. A servant came in and said, "We're going to die," and Elisha responded, "O sovereign Lord, open up his eyes." What eyes was Elisha talking about? The servant's eyes were open in the natural. He could see armies coming down on them, but he didn't have the spiritual eyes to see what God was going to do. Elisha, however, was seeing with spiritual eyes. He saw the divine protection that was on the way so he prayed for the servant's eyes to be opened in the same way. When the servant went back outside, he saw the divine protection all around them. (See 2 Kings 6:15-18.) Surely God didn't grow new eyeballs on the top of this guy's head. In answer to Elisha's prayer, the servant's spiritual eyes were opened. When Jesus says, "Let him who has eyes, let him see," He's not talking about our empirical knowledge. It's about more than what we see or hear physically. Until we get beyond our five senses, we can be in Christ but live as orphans all the days of our lives. The moment I learned to see things the way He sees them, everything changed. This same "sight" is available to you, in relationship with Him. Your life can change in one moment with one change in the way you see. I want *His* eyeballs, literally. I want to see from *His* perspective. I want to hear Him, to walk with Him every moment of my life. I want Him to correct me when I fall back to a place of seeing things through natural eyes instead of seeing through His eyes of love. He *is* love and I want to see others as He sees them.

I pray that we can all get to the place where we can say, "I am just on this earth to grow in revelation of who I am in God's family and to love others." If the Father created Adam to bless him, then I ought to be blessing people wherever I go. God's aroma ought to be on me. When I know who I am, it's easier to love others. When true sons and daughters are around orphans, they bring them life. People tell me all the time, "Chad, you're funny, you're always laughing." I'm this way because I'm genuinely happy. I've done the depression thing. I've been there and I absolutely don't want to do that anymore. I have found my Father. His number-one Son is my big Brother. The Holy Spirit lives in me, and angels are always around me. I am invited to feast at our Father's family Table and I like it. Why would I ever want to live any other way? Why would you? This is not denial, it is faith. We *all* get to run. We *all* get to take our place at the Table. We *all* get to live a life of intimacy. We *all* have the opportunity. Sonship is available when we embrace Him.

CHAPTER TWO

PLEASE GOD, DON'T EVER LET THIS HAPPEN TO ME AGAIN

It came from nowhere. One moment I was sitting on the edge of my bed thinking about whatever six-year-olds think about, and the next moment my heart was pounding, my head hurt, and my thoughts were racing all over the map. Irrational ideas from what seemed like hell itself came shooting at me: *What if I die tonight? What if I hurt myself? What if I choke in my sleep? What if I go crazy? What if I never leave this room again? What if this terror in my mind never goes away?*

If you have had a panic attack, you understand the depth of confusion and terror it brings. Plus, panic attacks seem to come and go at will. You never know when one is coming, and you never know when it will end. But it does end, and new anxiety about when the next one will strike takes over. *Tick, tock, tick, tock.* You watch the hands of your internal clock and think, *Dear God, please don't let this happen to me again. Please.*

It was not until I was in college that I stumbled across an infomercial about the Midwest Center for Stress and Anxiety and discovered that there was help for overcoming anxiety, depression, and agoraphobia. But that was many years away. This day I was six years old and too scared to tell anyone what had happened. All I knew was that it was a living hell. I was sure something terrible was wrong with me. I remember waking up one night unable to breathe, feeling as though someone had his hands clenched over my throat trying to kill me.

God said early in the game that it is not good for man to be alone, and panic attacks have shown me how true that is. People with panic disorder feel alone primarily because it is so hard to describe what is happening. If your arm is broken, you can show people your cast. If you have the flu, you have certain symptoms that can be diagnosed. But when it comes to panic disorder, you cannot get your hands around it. When I was growing up, there was no such thing as Google or WebMD. Back then most people had no idea what panic attacks were.

Sometimes I felt so disconnected from my body I just sat down and cried. I could look at something on TV, and my mind would spiral out of control. I began to talk about not feeling right, and my parents took me to the hospital. I can still see the nurse's unsmiling face as she took my blood pressure. I wanted to crawl inside of a hole and sit for ten eternities. I felt scared, hopeless, agitated, nervous and chaotic.

The attacks continued as I got older. I was driving to play basketball one night when, all of a sudden, I had to pull the car over because I was filled with terror. I did not know what to call it. I did not know whom to talk to. I did not know what to do. When I turned 18, I could not take it anymore. I tried to explain to my parents how much I was hurting. As any good parent would, they sent me to my doctor, and he recommended medication. I went on Klonopin and Zoloft for depression and anxiety. Thus began a twelve-year journey of coping with panic through chemicals.

I hurt for people who have to take medication. I never judge anyone for it. At that point in my life, I could not see any other way out of the pain. The drugs calmed my mind but left me feeling lethargic. I slept a lot. I felt in many ways that I had lost who I was. When I was in college, I kept the pill bottles on the shelf of my chest of drawers in my dorm room. Every time I took those pills, I thought, *I can't believe I am so weak that I have to take something to help me through the day.* My self-esteem took a nosedive. I felt that I had to explain my struggles and inferiority to others around me. The truth was that people had their own issues to deal with, and generally did not care that I was on medication. For me, however, it was the biggest deal in the world.

Shame invaded my life, and as the shame increased, so did the clinical depression. It is like a huge black cloud that follows your thoughts 24 hours a day. Even when you sleep you dream about it. It is as though you can never escape the spiral of negativity that grips your soul.

When I pray for people with clinical depression, I often get very emotional about their pain because I remember what that was like. I pray that as long as I live Jesus gives me opportunities to help people get set free. I hurt for people who are silently struggling with their own personal hells and think there is no way out. One day, I told my mom as we were walking into my doctor's office, "God will use this to help people some day." Now as I travel and speak about my story, men and women come up to me and say, "Thank God there is someone who struggles with the same thing, who understands."

My battle with panic disorder began to ebb and flow. There were some good seasons and some not so good seasons. Just when I thought I had whipped it, it reared its head. Even as I was writing this book and reflecting on my past, I had a three-week stretch when I battled anxiety. You would think that someone who is writing a book on the supernatural would just "suck it up and trust God," but that has not been my experience at all. It is possible to struggle with the messiness of life and see the supernatural at the same time. We all have our battles; this was mine. But in the midst of these tough days, I started to get glimpses that I was not alone. I also began to experience strange things.

MY PENTECOST

In the summer of 1996, I was preaching at a summer-long sports camp when a friend of mine handed me a book on the Holy Spirit. I was highly skeptical of the book and read it mainly to be able to dismantle it. Instead, it dismantled me. It created such hunger inside me for Jesus Christ that I did not know what to do. In a dorm room in Campbellsville, Kentucky, I said out loud, "I don't want to talk about Him this summer. I don't want to preach about Him. I want Him to walk through that door right there."

For three days, my spirit was fully alive, and I could not stop thinking about the Lord. One night that week, my team was watching the movie *Dead Man Walking*. Toward the end of the movie, I heard an audible voice in my right ear say, *Go to your room*. I got up and started toward my room. As I made my way across the campus, I could tell something unusual was about to happen. It was as though someone was walking with me. It is hard to explain. I had a sense that I should brace myself.

When I got into my room, I fell on the floor as though I weighed a ton and started weeping. The power and presence of God was so thick that I honestly thought I was going to die. I have never been more overwhelmed in my life. This was not a "time of reflection" where I contemplated the Lord. I wept and felt completely overwhelmed. I think it must have been the way Isaiah felt when he experienced the raw power and glory of God. After a while a friend came looking for me and as soon as he walked into the room he collapsed onto the floor and started weeping, too.

Even in the middle of that experience, I could not believe how intense it was. I would even use the word *terrifying* to explain it. Yet I was not afraid. How can something be terrifying but not make me afraid? I cannot say. Jesus' presence was consuming beyond my ability to describe it. Even three days after that experience I was exhausted from it. My sides were sore from crying and my eyes puffy. It was intense to say the least. I think many of us feel disqualified to experience God in out-of-the-box ways because we are aware of our own inadequacies, and we believe that they will keep us from experiencing

Him. Reading the Bible encourages me because the people God interacted with had struggles as well.

Even though I still struggle with panic disorder from time to time, that encounter transformed my ministry. The power of God fueled me to preach. He became real to me that night and I knew in some way I would never again preach without a fire in my belly. I also found that I grew more and more comfortable talking about my struggles, especially when I discovered how many people struggled with the same thing. I cringe when I hear of people being wounded by "faith" preachers who condemn others for any shortcomings in their journeys with Jesus. That is not the Jesus I have gotten to know. Depression and panic attacks do not seem to keep Jesus at a distance in my life. He actually seems to be drawn to brokenness.

WENDY

We all have stories of how we met our spouse. Let me just preface my story by saying that I am a seriously blessed man to be married to Wendy. The first night Wendy and I went out together with a group of friends, I knew something was special about her. She was different in a good kind of way. It was obvious that she took her relationship with Jesus very seriously. She was funny, witty, and beautiful. I on the other hand was not in a good place. My only interests as a 21-year-old were watching football, playing video games, and eating multiple boxes of Chef Boyardee on a daily basis. But suddenly, it was time to dream big.

To be clear, Wendy was not interested in me. I cannot blame her. At that time I was in a stage of wearing sweatpants, orange boots, and the same hoodie sweatshirt every day. I was her "safe" fat friend who hung out with her after she went on dates with other guys. I was a sensitive listener and I loved Jesus. We could wind up laughing and crying all in one setting. Little did I know that that would prove to be the secret for hitting the jackpot for life. It was genius.

I see young guys all the time trying to impress their potential lady friends by acting as though they have everything together. Recently I had a conversation with a friend I will call Stan. It went like this: "Stan, you are going about it all wrong. Instead of trying to impress her with how great you are, let her see you be tender. Allow her to know that you are not a Spirit-filled John Wayne." Stan knew that he could not ignore what I was saying. If you saw me with my wife, you would wonder what my secret is\ too.

Stan said to me, "I don't know how to do that." I responded, "Then you will stay single until Jesus Christ comes back to earth." I am not sure if Stan got the message, but I did, because my only hope with Wendy was to be genuine.

For six months, I spent time with Wendy as a friend. She dated some of my friends, and I dated Papa John's pizza. She went out on dates and would come over to my house to talk about the Lord, what was going on in her life, and anything else that college kids talk about. I started noticing that these sessions were increasing rapidly. My lightning-fast mind finally figured something out: I had the chance of a lifetime and I was completely blowing it.

One night Wendy left my house around 3 a.m. after another long session of talking through life's difficulties and challenges.

After she left, I told my college roommate, "You are looking at the Man in the Mirror. Michael Jackson sang it and I am about to live it. I'm about to make a change." Desperate times call for desperate measures. The next morning, I woke up and headed to Kmart to buy the unthinkable—a treadmill. Fatty was about to shock the world. I looked in the mirror that morning and said, "It's time for you to pay the piper, Pony Boy. No more fat college junior. The woman of your dreams is in your hands and you are going to lose her if you don't lose your gut." I got the treadmill and an infomercial special called the Gutbuster and started to lose some pounds. Things were changing. I went from wearing sweatpants, orange boots, and a lasagna-laced sweatshirt to khakis, Polo shirts, and nice shoes. My roommate thought I had gone mad, but I knew I was on the right path.

I could sense that Wendy knew something was up. Normally I smelled like a Philly cheesesteak, but now I smelled like the men's department at Macy's. The weight was coming off, and my inner James Bond was emerging. I was about to be the man of my best friend's dreams. At least, that's how it was playing out in my mind. The turning point was only a few days ahead. Visions of Casanova danced around in my mind as I formed my plan. I would woo this incredible woman of God and convince her to hop into my gladiator chariot and head off on an expedition of changing the world for God—or something like that. Here was my plan: invite Wendy over for a spaghetti dinner (spaghetti dinners are always more romantic). Kick my roommate out for the night. Turn on some Boyz II Men slow music. Kiss her. This was the plan, and I was going to execute it to perfection. That was, until the big night actually happened. Things like this never quite go down like you planned.

When Wendy got to my apartment, she looked at me like something was wrong. She could not figure out why the place was so clean. My apartment had not been cleaned in at least a year. On this night, however, it was apparent that something very important was about to go down. Wendy asked, "Why are you so dressed up? Are you OK?" I decided this was the moment that would reshape my story, so I went for it. I replied, "Before you leave here tonight, I'm going to kiss you." Webster defines the word awkward as, "causing difficulty, hard to deal with, causing or feeling embarrassment or inconvenience." I define awkward as that moment. Calling it awkward is actually the biggest understatement of my life. It was more awkward than a pregnant pole vaulter as Wendy and I stared at each other.

Wendy started laughing and said, "Are you kidding or being serious?" I said, "I'm being dead serious. It's going down." When we get to heaven, I'm going to ask God for a top 10 most awkward list of first kisses between couples who ended up getting married. I'll bet you a 100 bucks Wendy and I are on the list. The kiss lasted about fifteen seconds, and she left. I sat on my couch and thought, *What just happened?* When she got home, she called me, and we both agreed that it was stranger than a Tim Burton movie.

Twenty years later, I still laugh about our awkward start. We have three kids, a mortgage, and a natural gas bill. Things worked out to say the least. We've been in active ministry from the very beginning of our marriage and now we pastor The Garden Greenville Church. Over the years we've had some ups and downs, just like any other married couple. Six years ago, we had our biggest down yet when we hit the first crisis in our marriage, which I'll talk about more later. I had no idea God would use it to lead us to a greater understanding of how grace produces literal transformation. It happens not only in marriages, but also in the Supernatural when we pray for people, because grace flows through vulnerability. And vulnerability marks our lives when we're locked in at the Table.

SEMINARY

I graduated from college and after one summer of preaching, God told me clearly that I was supposed to go to Beeson Divinity School in Birmingham, Alabama, on the campus of Samford University. That idea had to be from God because I never in a million years wanted to attend seminary. My dad told his friends that I was planning to go to "The Seminary," which made me laugh. He still seems to think that there is one seminary in the world where all the preachers get herded like sheep.

Seminary was also a stretch for me because of my college experience. Like many college students, I was lazy with my study habits. My grades stank. I put most of my focus on watching a very average football team at the University of Georgia because I was brainwashed at an early age about the Bulldogs. Most anyone growing up in Georgia is raised to be Georgia Bulldogs. "Bulldog born, Bulldog bred, and when we die, we'll be Bulldog dead." I am now passing that on to my children. Add to that my incredible roommate Chris "Block" Lynch who specialized in cooking. Instead of studying, I ate my way to a 1.9 GPA. And I dated Papa John's for a couple of years before God intervened and brought my amazing wife across my path.

The funny thing is, I was feeling good before the bad news came. I remember well the letter from the admissions director at Beeson. It was addressed to "William," which is my first name. It is never good when someone calls me "William." The letter said, "Dear William, your grades stank at Georgia, and God hates you, so our answer is no." These were not the exact words, but that is what it sounded like to me. My parents had already bought a cake and balloons to celebrate. This was not a good situation. After I read the letter, I walked to my room, got on my knees and told God, "You called me to go to Beeson. I don't know what to do. It's Your problem, not mine."

I could not articulate it then, but I somehow trusted that this rejection was not my problem. After all, I did not call myself to seminary. God did. So in my mind, it was His responsibility and not my burden to carry. During that time, my parents bought a house from a pastor named Benny who was moving to Birmingham to pastor a church there. Not long after I prayed about getting rejected from God's school, our phone rang. It was Benny. He introduced himself and asked if he could speak to my parents. Before I passed the phone along, I asked him if he had any connections at Beeson since he was now a pastor in Birmingham. Benny said that, as a matter of fact, he was just about to have lunch with the dean. When I heard this,

I said, "Beeson told me that I can't go to school there. Is there any way you could put in a good word for me?"

Within about a day, Beeson's admission's director called me and said, "The dean would like to give you a chance to prove yourself. Welcome to the Beeson family." So one bright morning with our dog, Millie, we took off on I-85 South pulling a U-Haul. Two professors, Dr. Robert Smith Jr. and Dr. Calvin Miller, were waiting for me. I had never heard of either one of them and they sure had never heard of me. Yet by God's design, these two men would redirect the course of my life. I know it sounds a little dramatic to say it like that, but that is exactly what happened.

Wendy and I settled into seminary life. Some friends from our church were in the same apartment complex. We called it our own little Melrose Place. God opened the door for me to pastor college students at The Church at Brook Hills in Birmingham. I had a good rhythm of school and work for a few years as I helped Christian students work through their college obsession with Calvinism. I like John Calvin. I even hacked my way through his *Institutes of the Christian Religion* while I was in seminary. But sometimes I feel as though I need a vacation after a conversation with a passionate Calvinist. I was given a grace to help students exhale as they hammered out their own theology.

While I was at Beeson, a mentor asked me if I had ever considered having counseling. I did consider it, and it was one of the best decisions I would ever make.

THE BACKSIDE OF THE DESERT

Let me state this bluntly: up until this point, for a long time I hated God. I never had a problem with Jesus, but I thought His Father was the epitome of meanness. I was working toward my master's in divinity and I hated God. It took counseling to lead me to this revelation. Can you imagine how shocked I was? To get back to the point where I had first started to hate God required eye-opening counseling sessions and long conversations with my wife and friends. That era seems foreign now because all I do is minister the love of the Father as I pray for the sick, broken and hurting. But it was not foreign then. Now, as a middle-aged pastor, I am slow to trust anyone who has not been through some form of counseling. That is because my counselors served as consultants to my soul. They pointed out things in me that I had never thought about before. Counseling was so helpful for me that I wondered how I made it so long without it. But that is not to say it was easy. I am sure there were many times my wife thought, *God, why did You lead me to this man?*

I meet people all the time who want to have positions of godly authority like Moses, yet very few want to go to the backside of the desert. Many of us would like to have the impact Paul did, but who wants to be shipwrecked, stoned, bitten by a snake, and persecuted by the religious establishment? Joseph has a great story, but who in the world wants to go through thirteen years in a pit or in slavery or in prison? Yet you will be hard-pressed to find anyone in the Bible who made a great impact for the Kingdom without going through the wringer. To be great at what the Father has called you to be great at, you have to know who you are; difficult times and good counselors reveal that.

Jesus went into the desert, and I have a hard time believing that He loved every second of it. I generally want to backhand the person who came up with the proverb, "Our biggest breakdowns lead to our biggest breakthroughs." But that person is right. And that truth hurts. Even in seasons when it looks as though satan is winning his war against us, the Father has a way of turning those seasons into beauty.

CHAPTER THREE

AT THE KING'S TABLE

God never wanted Israel to have a king. He set up a leadership structure and put judges and prophets in charge, but the Israelites looked around and saw that other nations had a king, so they started asking for a king. Then they pushed and pushed. Sometimes, when you push God hard enough and long enough, He'll give you what you don't need. As a pastor, I can't tell you how many times I have seen people take their lives and destinies into their own hands only to find out that it is never wise to make plans and then ask God to bless those plans. The wiser statement is, "Father, show me what you want me to do and I'll be just fine with that." The Israelites kept pushing and God said, "Okay. This is not going to go well, but I'm making Saul your king."

When God predicts something, He has a remarkable track record of being right. So it was with Saul, Israel's first king. To make a very long story short, Saul ended up being a very ungodly king. As a result, God anointed David to become the next king. David was probably 12 years old when Samuel first anointed him as king. Then he went back to what he was doing.

It was not his time. Saul was insanely jealous and tried, for a long time, to kill David. This proved difficult in part because Saul's son, Jonathan, was David's best friend. Jonathan saved David from Saul more than once. David promised Jonathan he would take care of his family should Jonathan die before him. Jonathan and Saul were both killed in battle and David became king of Judah when he was 30 years old.

Now picture in your mind King David, enjoying feasts at the king's table, thriving in leadership. Israel had 40 years of peace and prosperity, and it was amazing. Perhaps David was telling stories of the old days and reminiscing about his friend Jonathan when he suddenly remembered his promise to Jonathan —that his family would be well taken care of. And they were, except for Jonathan's son Mephibosheth, who was lame in both feet. Mephibosheth lived in Lo-debar, the land of barrenness. David knew he must keep his promise even though Mephibosheth didn't even know the promise existed. An invitation went out from the palace to Mephibosheth, inviting him to come and sit at the King's table. I'm guessing he was surprised. Being invited to the king's table meant he would be taken care of until the day he died, or until the king was overthrown. He would be treated like a son. All of this actually happened to Mephibosheth. King David also restored to him the land that was his inheritance and gave him overseers to work the land on his behalf. That's a pretty good deal.

So, was Mephibosheth overjoyed by this amazing turn of events? Not so much. He reacted by saying "What is your servant, that you should notice a dead dog like me?" (2 Samuel 9:8b). If we pay attention long enough to our own words, and the words of friends around us, we tend to give signs of our own orphanhood with our words. Out of the mouth, the heart speaks. (See Luke 6:45.) Mephibosheth had known what it was like to be fatherless, to be without, to rely on others. This is all he knew. He knew how to fight to exist. He knew how to fight to belong. Instead of focusing on the goodness of the King, Mephibosheth focused on the fact that he was crippled, and on his own sense of unworthiness.

I believe with my entire heart that satan's number-one tactic is condemnation. Martin Luther called Romans 8, "The Gateway to the Bible." I find it interesting that the first verse of Romans 8 is, *"Therefore, there is now no condemnation for those who are in Christ Jesus."* (NIV). Not much has changed since the days of Mephibosheth. It seems the biggest battle we go through is our own sense of unworthiness. I started walking in the prophetic 15 years ago and I have found that self-condemnation this is the number one reason people have a hard time stepping into the reality of First Corinthians 14:1. It's practically impossible to walk in a high level of the prophetic or any other gift and at the same time develop a critical spirit towards yourself.

Picture what it must have been like for Mephibosheth. His grandfather was the first king of Israel, and his dad was the best friend of the current king. Yet, he was living without any of those benefits. He did not know what it was like to be invited into a family. He was uncomfortable at the king's table and wanted to return to Lo-debar, the land of barrenness, the place where he felt more comfortable. He wanted to return to the familiar. In those biblical days, his physical ailment was looked upon as a sign of weakness and worthlessness. He had been groomed to see himself as the opposite of the opportunity that awaited him. His thinking was essentially "old covenant" thinking. Under the Old Covenant, the connection between God and man was tenuous at best.

BACK TO EDEN

Go with me now, in your mind, to the Upper Room. Jesus and His disciples are gathered there to share what became known as the Last Supper. Jesus told His disciples He was going to institute a New Covenant, but they couldn't understand what he was saying. The Old Covenant between God and Moses had stood for thousands of years. Jesus was about to put a face on God, to show us the character of His Father. He came to reconnect us to the Father, to invite us to the King's Table. He was about to make a way so that we can have deep friendship with our Father in a relationship where we will be taken care of, where angels minister to us and protect us. He was opening the door for us to go back to a place of intimacy with the Father, who is Provider and Protector. Jesus was giving us back our inheritance.

Just as Mephibosheth was brought to the king's table because of the promise made by David to Jonathan, so are we invited to the King's Table because of the promise of the New Covenant that comes through Jesus Christ. That's good news! In fact, that's awesome news! Just like Mephibosheth, we can eat at the King's Table all our days. We can enjoy the benefits of being a son. We can enjoy His kindness. For me, these are not just hyper spiritual words that are full of passion with no substance. I remember what it was like to be in a fetal position in my kitchen at age 28, with zero ability to ever believe that I would one day become good friends with the God that I was convinced was always upset with me.

The narrative of the Bible is actually an invitation back into Eden. It's an invitation back into close and intimate friendship with God. People who are looking to walk in a high level of power in the Kingdom, where healing and miracles are not just things to be studied in the Bible, are people who must settle on this conversation deep inside of their own hearts. Friendship with God comes with great benefits. Healing and the prophetic flow out of a deep and intimate connection with Him. I have noticed over the years that all of my power encounters in the Kingdom—when I have seen people delivered of demons, healed, and given shockingly accurate words of knowledge—have come from my revelation that I'm in Eden with the Father. He loves me as much as He loves Jesus Christ. This is the baseline for friendship with God. This is the baseline for a powerful life in the prophetic, where the ability to hear His voice is not predicated by me having to go to someone else to receive. We need to be raising up the next generation as men and women, sons and daughters who are getting words directly from Abba. He's our Father according to Jesus. When we settle this idea of Eden in our mind, it's the launching pad for explosive growth in our ability to hear Him for ourselves.

LIVE BY FAITH

Very few people are comfortable receiving blessing. I truly believe that the highest form of pride is the inability to receive. We tend to think that we don't deserve intimacy or protection.

Like Mephibosheth, instead of focusing on the goodness of the King, we focus on our own inadequacies, unworthiness, and handicaps. Spiritual orphans are more comfortable in Lo-debar, the land of barrenness, than at the King's Table.

Let's get very practical here. Do you fight for your place at the King's Table? Do you think people have a plan to remove you? Are you always a victim? Do you blame others? I know it is hard to truly ask yourself those questions. If you are like me, and you are desperate for more than a promise of one day going to heaven, desperate to leave spiritual orphanhood behind, you will ask the hard questions and face the hard facts. What is the answer for this spiritual orphanhood? How is it healed? What's the cure? Is it to spend more time thinking about our past, our injustices, our unworthiness and depravity? It may seem a sign of deep faith to focus on our sin—but that's the enemy's spin. Satan, the accuser, wants us to believe we belong in Lo-debar. Our Dad invites us to His Table. He wants us to live as a son or daughter, in the Family, with all the benefits. It takes faith to live this way. Faith is the currency of heaven. You have to believe you are a son. It is by faith we are saved, it is by faith we receive Holy Spirit, and it is by faith we learn to live with Him. Sons and daughters talk about who they are in Christ, and what He has done. Orphans talk about who they are *not* and what they have done. Spiritual orphans constantly want to earn approval. They want to satisfy their own appetites. They need others to constantly affirm them. They get their identity from the viewpoint of others.

Those of us who follow Christ will be tempted for the rest of our lives to follow Mephibosheth's lead and to drift back to Lo-debar. Throughout our lives, we tend visit the King's Table on Sunday and drift back to Lo-debar the rest of the week. Then we drift back to the King's Table and do it all again. We get our fix on Sunday mornings, then we move back to orphan thinking. I don't want to live that way. I want to live my life at the King's Table. I want to be so determined to stay there that if someone tries to pull me away, I will simply not tolerate it. No one can pull me away without risking a punch to the face. I won't allow anything to make me return to Lo-debar. I will not leave the Table.

As you come up against satan the accuser, you have to choose how you are going to view your life. Are you going to view your life based on your own thoughts, on what others say about you, on what the enemy says about you, or on what the Father says about you? The battle you will face for the rest your life will be the battle between Lo-debar and the King's Table. It will be an ongoing fight to resist the pull to be more comfortable in Lo-debar than to remain at the Table. It seems noble, but it's not. At the King's Table, you hear the thoughts of your Father, the King, and all other voices grow dim. When you're sitting at the King's Table stuffing your face full of His food, and enjoying intimacy with Father, Son, and Holy Spirit, it's hard to hear the enemy. This makes it hard for me to understand why so many believers are so demon-centric. It's shocking how often I hear about what the enemy is doing in the lives of believers. Perhaps the enemy's voice is loud and clear because believers don't actually sit at the Table with their Father, Jesus, and Holy Spirit. Hearing the voice of the enemy constantly may not be a call to warfare intercession, it may be a sign that you've left the King's Table and returned to Lo-debar. You have allowed your thoughts to be permeated with lack.

One of the most amazing healings I have ever seen in my life was in Missouri when I prayed for a friend's knee. As I prayed for him, at least 50 flies started flying around his head. My friend received a miracle right in front of our eyes. His mcl and acl were torn, and something in his ankle was torn. In front of our eyes, his knee began to shake when I commanded it to be whole. We watched what looked like a vein underneath his skin, from his ankle to his knee, move. It happened so fast that we were astonished. The enemy is more real than you think he is. He buzzes about like a fly, but he is just a maggot. The Father's Table always trumps that maggot. The accuser is under your feet. Why reach down, pull him up, eyeball-to-eyeball, and entertain his thoughts? I felt like I got born again, again when I came to my senses (see Luke 15:17) and decided I wasn't going to make one more single excuse as to why I can't live in Eden the rest of my life while on this earth. I took responsibility for my own thoughts and my own life. It's more fun to be a friend of God than a victim of the enemy. Make your decision to get acclimated at the King's Table and receive the feast of intimacy with Him. You may be surprised at how fast you grow in your ability to hear the voice of your Father. You belong.

CHAPTER FOUR

BELIEVING AND BELONGING

E veryone longs to belong. In fact the need to belong is so strong that people will do almost anything to satisfy it. Young people join violent gangs out of a need to belong. Many who are involved in the occult got to that dark place out of a sense of rejection, of not belonging. Our need to belong seems to be part of our DNA, perhaps because God designed us to belong to Him, to His family. He made a place for us at His Table before the foundations of the world. Satan is always busy trying to get us away from our place at the Table. To get to the King's Table and stay there, we must believe what God has said. The message of the Kingdom is not to say "yes" to heaven, it is to say "yes" to the King. He is our Lord, our creator, and more than that, He has invited us into His family. In God's family, Jesus is our big Brother. He isn't just the bridge to heaven, He's the bridge to the Father. When you understand and embrace these truths you realize that the invitation is to come and enjoy God, to walk with Him in the cool of the day—to just be with Him. When is the last time you just enjoyed God? Wouldn't you like to spend your life enjoying God rather than wondering every day if He even likes you? You can, if you believe.

When you truly believe that His Table is your home, you get to experience things in the Kingdom that others don't. The supernatural becomes natural to you—and you live in thankfulness for the place you have at the Table. It's not a place of arrogance. It's a place of belonging. I know this because I've lived it. I've lived in Lo-debar and I do not want to go back. I spent much of my life hating God because I did not understand Him. I have to tell you—I am no longer Mephibosheth. I am not in Lo-debar. I am God's child. I don't say this because I am a pastor. I don't even let my church call me "pastor." I'm just Chad. I sit at the Table because it's where I belong. This is home to me now. My goal for you is that you will leave Lo-debar and come home. Come to your place at the Table.

Living at home at the Table means things that once would have seemed strange and impossible become the usual. Imagine that an angel manifests to you and instead of being terrified, you calmly say, "How's it going?" I'm not kidding. This is life at the King's Table. Dramatic things can happen to you spiritually and not catch you off guard. What if your eyes were trained so that the realm of the supernatural was more real than what you can see, feel, or taste? Imagine you own your own business and business is not going well. You've had four prophetic words in the past month about how well your business is going to go. When the King's Table is home, instead of falling apart, you can hang onto the Word of God, believing in Him. We need to understand that the Word from the Lord is more real than the

42

bank account that is precariously close to zero dollars. It is more real than our lack. How do we go about believing in God? It's a learning process. You begin to trust Him beyond your own understanding, and as you do, He becomes your reality.

It is awesome when things manifest as He promised and instead of being shocked, you think, "Well, that is what You said would happen, Father." This is how Jesus responded to satan in the desert. He repeatedly referenced the Word He believed. Over and over He responded to satan beginning with the words "It is written." The same naturally supernatural lifestyle that Jesus lives at the King's Table is possible for all sons and daughters of the King. We don't have to live like spiritual orphans. We can move beyond doubt to belief and take our place at the Table of the King.

EMBRACING HEAVEN'S CULTURE

When confronted with doubt, spiritual orphans say, "You are so right, it is so true." Spiritual sons say, "hush." Waiting for doubt to leave is ridiculous. You don't wait for it to leave—you tell it to hush. Chapter 1 in the gospel of Luke is a good place to see the difference between doubt, which is a characteristic of a spiritual orphan, and belief, which is a characteristic of a spiritual son or daughter. Please understand, there's nothing wrong with doubt as long as you don't yield to it. Faith is not the absence of doubt. Faith is looking at doubt, punching it in the face and moving towards the truth. If you wait until there's no doubt, you will be waiting for Jesus Christ to come back. He will split the sky open and you will be sitting there saying, "wait a minute."

In Luke 1:5-25 we meet Zechariah, who was a priest in the lineage of Abijah, and his wife Elizabeth who was barren. He and his wife were very old, and both were righteous in the sight of God, observing all His commands and decrees blamelessly. Being a priest, he had a strong history with God and was very familiar with Him. Simply put, God liked this guy. On this particular day, Zechariah was serving as a priest before God. He was chosen, according to the custom of the priesthood, to go to the temple of the Lord and burn incense. When the time for the burning of incense came, all the assembled worshipers were praying outside. This was not just a few people showing up for church. This was a big deal. Zechariah went in, and they were all outside waiting to see what would happen. No one expected what happened next. An angel of the Lord appeared to Zechariah, standing at the right side of the altar of incense.

Think about this for a minute. God released an angel to personally deliver a message to Zechariah, a righteous man who had a history with God and was very familiar with Him. Isn't it a bit odd that someone so familiar with God, who had been around the ways of God for so long (remember Zechariah was old) would react the way he did—with doubt? The angel delivered 11 amazing promises to Zechariah. *"Your wife Elizabeth will bear you a son, and you are to call him John. He will be a joy and a delight to you, and many will rejoice because of his birth, for he will be great in the sight of the Lord. He is never to take wine or other fermented drink, and he will be filled with the Holy Spirit even before he is born. He will bring back many of the people of Israel to the Lord their God. And he will go on before the Lord, in the spirit and power of Elijah, to turn the hearts of the parents to their children and the disobedient to the wisdom of the righteous—to make ready a people prepared for the Lord"* (Luke 1:13-17 NIV). That's a lot of promises. How many more promises does a righteous man need to hear? You'd think Zechariah would have jumped for joy and thankfulness. Yet, in the very next verse, he asked the angel, *"How can I be sure of this? I am an old man and my wife is well along in years"* (Luke 1:18 NIV). He doubted the word! We know that we are growing in deep friendship with God when an encounter happens, or a strong word is given, and we believe what the Father is saying regardless of how this affects our natural senses. We simply default to childlike belief.

Jesus was the perfect example of someone who lived believing what the Father said. In fact He only did what He saw the Father doing, only said what He heard the Father saying. When He raised Lazarus from the grave, He didn't even pray for him. Instead, He said, "Father this is for You, not for Me." Then He simply said, "Get up." (See John 11:41-42.) When a little boy from a crowd of 5,000 handed Jesus a few fish and loaves of bread, Jesus was just messing with Philip when He said, *"Where shall we buy bread for these people to eat?"* (John 6:5 NIV). He already knew His Father would provide more than enough. He wasn't mortified by anything down here on earth. People were constantly plotting to kill Him, but He was so connected to Father that even constant death threats didn't impact the way He operated.

You know where you are in relation to Lo-debar based upon your reaction to the manifestations of the Kingdom of God.

Why are we so shocked when someone is healed? Why are we so shocked when someone gets delivered? Why are we so shocked when the presence of God fills the room and we literally cannot stand up under the power? It should be so common. For Zechariah, it didn't happen that way. Many times, it doesn't happen that way for us, either. If you're wondering where you are on the scale between Lo-debar and the King's Table, ask yourself this question: "When you are squeezed in a "suddenly moment," what comes out?" What are suddenly moments? The gospels and the book of Acts are full of suddenly moments—moments when the unexpected happens and people must react immediately. You can gauge where you are with God when a suddenly moment happens. If you squeeze an orange, apple juice doesn't come out. Yet, when you squeeze a born-again Christian, many times, more of the enemy than the Kingdom comes out. If I squeeze you in Lo-debar, then Lo-debar comes out. If I squeeze you at the King's Table, sonship will come out.

Spiritual orphans are always dominated by what they can see, taste, touch, feel, and hear. Those at the King's Table trust His Word no matter what the natural says, because the Word matters more than what we can taste, touch, feel, and hear. This is why Paul says, in Colossians 3:1-3, to set your heart on things above; set your mind on things above. What if heaven's culture was more real to you than the earth? It can happen if you will fight through doubt with faith, and believe.

Let's return to Zechariah. Gabriel showed up and Zechariah was thrown into doubt. In a suddenly moment he wasn't able to set his mind on things above. Zechariah asked the angel, "How can I be sure of this?" He was actually talking to a mighty angel of God and giving into unbelief. This did not make Gabriel or God very happy. *"I am Gabriel,"* was the response. *"I stand in the presence of God, and I have been sent to speak to you and to tell you this good news. And now you will be silent and not able to speak until the day this happens, because you did not believe my words, which will come true at their appointed time"* (Luke 1:19-20 NIV). I can just imagine Gabriel taking his sword and putting it right up to Zechariah's nose and saying something like, "You do *not* want to say this to Jehovah." You see, God values your belief. He wants you to believe and receive what's at His Table, not doubt it and do without for the rest of your life. Orphans will focus on their doubt while sons push past their doubt and believe. It isn't that sons are more favored or holy, it's simply that they believe. They counter doubt with faith. Without faith, it is impossible to believe. Living in that place of "in all faith believing" takes courage.

So, what is faith? Many believers struggle to understand it. We already know that faith is not the absence of doubt. Faith is punching doubt right in the face and continuing to move forward. Faith is believing God and taking Him at His Word no matter what the natural realm says. Faith says, "No one is taking me off my place at the Table—no angels, no demons, no nothing." When you're living in faith at the King's Table, you don't need a great man or woman of God to anoint you. You were anointed at Calvary. All you have to do is agree with Calvary. To the degree you agree with Calvary, you lock onto the truth. When you lock onto the truth you will find yourself being wooed to the Table and eventually, it will feel like home. When you're solidly at home with God you don't get easily shaken. If someone gives you a bizarre prophetic word, you don't fall apart. Instead, you say, "Thank you so much for giving me that word, but that's not from Father. I don't judge you. I love you." An orphan's response is different. When an orphan hears a bizarre word, their response is, "Ugghhh, destruction is coming to me." In contrast, sons and daughters say, "Surely goodness and mercy shall follow me all the days of my life." I'm encouraging you to exercise your faith for yourself, to make God's truths so personal that you literally believe you're as close to the heart of Father as Jesus was while He was here. I'm talking about believing. I love how Luke didn't spend too much time focusing on Zechariah's doubts. The gospel narrative goes on to tell us that even though Zechariah doubted, Elizabeth got pregnant, just as promised. The truth is, God keeps His promises.

RESPONDING TO GOD'S PURSUIT

Zechariah and Elizabeth were not the only ones who experienced a suddenly moment that demanded a faith response. There was also Mary. Mary was a very young girl. Biblical scholars estimate her age to be about 13 or 14 years old. She was a young girl from a no-name town in the middle of nowhere, called Nazareth. God being no respecter of persons sent Gabriel to this desolate location with the most astounding and impactful message the world has ever known. *"In the sixth month of Elizabeth's pregnancy, God sent the angel Gabriel to Nazareth, a town in Galilee, to a virgin pledged to be married to a man named Joseph, a descendant of David. The virgin's name was Mary. The angel went to her and said, 'Greetings you who are highly favored! The Lord is with you.' Mary was greatly troubled at his words and wondered what kind of greeting this might be"* (Luke 1:26-29 NIV). Mary was troubled by the magnitude of the good news, not the news itself. Zechariah was full of doubt. Mary was full of faith and incredulous all at the same time. Often, when God shows up, those who don't know His true nature expect that He just wants to rough them up or teach them a lesson. Imagine if an angel manifested to you and just said, "Father loves you so much"? Remember the angel that appeared to Cornelius and simply said, *"Your prayers and gifts to the poor have come up as a memorial offering before God"* (Acts 10:4 NIV). A paraphrase of that verse is "God really likes you." These kinds of suddenly moments are amazing, especially when people respond with faith.

Gabriel brought *the* Good News and Mary responded in faith. "But the angel said to her, *"Do not be afraid, Mary; you have found favor with God. You will conceive and give birth to a son, and you are to call him Jesus. He will be great and will be called the Son of the Most High. The Lord God will give him the throne of His father David"* (Luke 1:30-32 NIV). Can you even imagine the magnitude of these words for Mary? This was a huge message, delivered pretty matter-of-factly by Gabriel. I love how, to God, things down here are just not a big deal. That is the whole story of the Bible. God was always using ordinary, unexpecting people to do extraordinary and amazing things, even things that seemed impossible. Here is a nugget to hold onto. God chooses us. He's the one doing the choosing. Our choice becomes simple. It's either yes or no. There is no other option, just yes or no.

One of the things I have noticed is how many times God pursues people for an assignment. In Genesis 12:1-3, Abram was not praying that God would show up and ask him to be the father of a nation. As a matter of fact, he was living in a polytheistic society and culture, and there is a great chance Abram was not aware of Jehovah's identity. He likely didn't know who God was. Think on that for a minute. It was God's idea to initiate a relationship and assignment with Abram. Then there was Moses who was on the backside of a desert when God showed up in a burning bush. (See Exodus 3:1-17.) Moses never saw this coming, which continues to show me why Richard Foster calls God, "The great hound of heaven." (See *Prayer: Finding the Heart's True Home*, page 70.) Jesus is the one who finds Andrew and tells him to go to his brother Simon Peter. (See John 1:41.) Once again God takes the initiative and people have to decide what to do in response.

I don't know what large words you have been given over your life, but nothing can compare to the words given to and received by Mary. Let's look more closely at how she handled it. She basically said, "Okay—well, how will this be? I am a virgin." (See Luke 1:34.) I love her response. It's certainly not full of doubt. Sometimes, when God shows up and you know it's Him, you need to just go ahead and believe before you take time to over analyze the word being given to you. If Mary had processed this word for too long, doubt could have crept in. She could have thought, "Wait a minute. God is going to be in my belly? God? No!" Mary didn't over analyze in the natural. She just received in her spirit what God was saying.

Gabriel wasn't finished. He continued, *"The Holy Spirit will come on you and the power of the Most High will overshadow you. So the holy one to be born will be called the Son of God"* (Luke 1:35 NIV). There's never been another message on this earth to a human being from God bigger than this message. Just look at Mary's response: *"I am the Lord's servant.... May your word to me be fulfilled"* (Luke 1:38). She basically said, "Sounds good to me. I'm all in." The very same angel, Gabriel, appeared to both Zechariah and Mary. Both received astounding words that seemed impossible in the natural. One said, "I just don't believe it." The other said, "Well, let it be done to me as you have spoken." You may be thinking, "No one ever prophesies over me. What word, exactly, am I supposed to believe?"

Are you ready? Let me prophesy over you. How about this for a prophetic word:

> John 1:12: *"Yet to all who did receive Him, to those who believed in his name, He gave the right to become children of God...."* Do you believe it? yes
>
> Ephesians 1:5: *"...he predestined us for adoption to sonship through Jesus Christ, in accordance with his pleasure and will...."* Do you believe it? yes
>
> Romans 15:7: *"Accept one another, then, just as Christ accepted you,* [just as Christ brought you to his King's Table], *in order to bring praise to God."* Do you believe it? yes
>
> First Corinthians 6:17: *"But whoever is united with the Lord is one with him in spirit."* Do you believe it? yes

Colossians 1:21-22: *"Once you were alienated from God and were enemies in your minds because of your evil behavior* [in Lo-debar]. *But now he has reconciled you* [He's bridged you] *by Christ's physical body through death to present you holy in his sight, without blemish and free from accusation..."* Do you believe it? yes

RECEIVING THE WHITE ROBE

My friend Justin had a major breakthrough when he finally believed one of these truths. I met Justin eight years ago, when he was a landscaper in Greenville, South Carolina. I wanted him to give me a quote for some landscaping we wanted done at our house. In our first meeting, a 30-minute quote turned into a 4-hour prophetic prayer time. On my back porch, the Lord began to show me things about Justin's life that were quite dramatic. The power of the prophetic is that the Holy Spirit opens up doors in one minute to show what sometimes takes years to discover by doing life with someone. To say that Justin and I bonded during that time on my back porch is putting it lightly. This began a six-year discipling relationship. I invited Justin into my life and began to invest a lot of time in helping him develop a paradigm of what it looks like to pursue Jesus with every inch of one's being.

A year into our time together, Justin shared with me that he was having a really difficult time hearing God at all. It was driving him crazy. He was getting tired of not being able to hear the voice of his Shepherd. (See John 10:27.) I decided to meet with him at Cracker Barrel. I love meeting over food, and thought that a nice, relaxing southern meal would put Justin in a great place to receive a challenging word from me. When we sat down, I said, "Justin, I am not going to leave this restaurant until you get a word from God for me. Time is up. It's time for you to start operating at a high level in the prophetic." He stared at me like something was wrong with me. A couple of hours passed, and Justin was not hearing anything. He was frustrated. So was I. We finally had to give up and leave the restaurant without a breakthrough.

That night Justin went to bed. In one dream, everything changed for him. In his dream, the Lord walked up to him and said, "You want to know why you can't hear me like Chad does?" Then the Lord showed Justin that he was dressed in a filthy garment that was gross. Justin looked at what he was dressed in and realized that it was dirty. Then the Lord handed him a robe that was pure white. The Lord said to him, "When you see yourself dressed in white like this and truly believe that you are clean in My eyes, you will hear Me."

I have been around very few people more prophetic than Justin. He went from not being able to hear God to hearing Him a mile a minute. It all changed with one simple principle: until you see yourself as being as clean as Jesus, you will never walk in a high level of the prophetic. It is practically impossible to be naturally supernatural if you see yourself as dirty in the Father's eyes. In other words, you cannot pull your chair up to the King's Table, and stay there, if you don't believe. Justin had to believe Colossians 1:21-22. He had to believe that, thanks to Jesus, he literally is pure and blameless before God. Truly

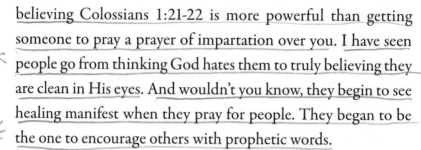

believing Colossians 1:21-22 is more powerful than getting someone to pray a prayer of impartation over you. I have seen people go from thinking God hates them to truly believing they are clean in His eyes. And wouldn't you know, they begin to see healing manifest when they pray for people. They began to be the one to encourage others with prophetic words.

Jesus gives lots of words, but very few people actually believe them. I am telling you, come sit at the Table and stay at the Table. You don't need a pastor to hug every Sunday morning. You don't need someone to affirm you nine times, just so you can get through the day. Take one passage and, for once in your life, decide to sit at the Table and stay at the Table. No matter what is happening in your life, you can stay connected to the Table because you believe God's Word. Others may ask, "How can you be so confident when it doesn't seem like things are going great in your life?" The answer is: "Because I believe God more than my circumstances."

Bottom line for my life: I would rather sit at His Table and have my life look like Lo-debar, than to have material abundance, but a soul full of Lo-debar. Isn't it interesting that in the middle of suffering Paul kept saying, "I just want to know you, I just want to know you." At His Table, even suffering produces the sweet aroma of intimacy. It may seem like everything's falling apart in my life, but I have something other people don't have. I've got sonship. I've got a Father. Lo-debar is no longer a place I want to be. So even when life gets tough, it doesn't force me away from the Table. I continue to dig into His Word and believe His Truths.

When I open the Word to just discover how good it is, I can grow more in six months than six years. If I'm studying to get to the King's Table, then I've already lost. If I believe I am already at the King's Table, and I am studying to realize what this means, then it makes sense to me when David says, *"You prepare a table before me in the presence of my enemies"* (Psalm 23:5). The Table doesn't give me immunity from spiritual warfare, it just equips me to take naps in the storms and wonder why other people are flipping out so much.

The King's Table is a good place to dwell. If you are tired of making your abode in Lo-debar, then get out. Don't be a string-bound elephant. Have you seen them? They are huge elephants who just sit there, not moving, because they are attached to a string, a little bitty string tied around a small 2 x 4 on the ground. When I see this, I want to say to the elephant, "You have the power to kill a village and you just sit right there. Just pull the thing out of the ground, just pull the thing out." If your thoughts are keeping you in the suburbs of Lo-debar, get some new thoughts. As Paul would say, "Quit drinking the milk, quit blaming your pastor who 15 years ago looked at you wrong, quit blaming the teacher who said you were ugly." We've all been hurt. We can all build libraries of doubt based upon our own experiences. Every once in a while, someone says, "I believe that word even if it never manifests." Then, they obey based on that truth. That's faith. It is an amazing experience. Think about where you are in relation to Lo-debar and the King's Table. Is it time for an about-face, to begin thinking like God thinks? Is it time to know the truth and act on it? Is it time to punch doubt in the face and keep moving forward? Is it time to believe?

CHAPTER FIVE

CHASING THE FATHER'S HEART

Have you ever asked what the Father wants from you? You will spend eternity with Him in heaven. The question we need to ask is, "What does He want here?" Let's begin with this—you are part of His family. He wants to do what families do, which is to enjoy being together. He wants to connect with you, to talk to you about things that you don't even think are that important. Spiritual orphans only go to God when crisis is on the line. Sons say, "Father, what is on your mind?"

Recently, as we was about to leave on vacation, a sister of mine from our church prayed over me. As soon as she began praying, Holy Spirit said, "Listen to her." She said I had a very large assignment during our time away. I wasn't being called to minister, and I wasn't being called to speak. My first thought was, "Thank You, Father, I love those kinds of assignments."

All I had packed was one pair of shorts, three shirts, a bathing suit, and a pre-season college football magazine. Not exactly what you would wear if you were planning on blessing people.

The grocery store was a tenth of a mile from our condo. All I planned to do was eat, stare at the ocean, and hang out with my wife and kids. The very thought of it felt like heaven to me. I knew the assignment that week was for my wife and I to connect on a deep level, to have lots of conversations. And we did. We talked all week and experienced a significant breakthrough. As a matter of fact, I don't remember having a week like that since we've been married. Our kids were there, there were no mediators, we were not reading any Christian books. I wasn't listening to teaching on marital interests. I love all that, but we just talked.

Then, I went for a walk on the beach and Father said, "Chad, because of your obedience to your assignment for this week, you have already opened doors for yourself that you know nothing of." I was walking from the condo and I asked, "What do you mean?" He answered, "So many people misunderstand me. I'm not a pushover. When I give someone an assignment in the Kingdom, I'm a rewarder of their obedience. I want you to start teaching how I'm a rewarder." You see, God doesn't play favorites. He doesn't just say, "Reward that one, don't reward that one." He wants us to believe and obey. Paul tells us multiple times that we should lean into obedience. Orphans always have a reason, an excuse as to why they can't be obedient, and why they just don't have it in them. A son or daughter says, "Lord, what is it you want with me? My life is yours. I have no right to the Table. I am grateful to be at the Table. I just want to be with You, to enjoy You. I'll do whatever You ask because I love You and want to please You." Blessings manifest when you go after the heart of Father, not after the heart of the blessing.

If you're fulfilling an assignment to get blessed, you're missing the whole point. Fulfill the assignment because you're chasing Father's heart.

LIFE IN THE PROMISED LAND

People respond differently to fear. My grandmother ran. She lived in one of those houses built in the fifties that had closets that are 6 miles long. Today we have walk-in-closets so big you could raise a family in them. There is something in me that loves to scare people. I would hide in my grandmother's closet in the mornings and when she opened that door to get her shoes, she would see me and take off running, no screams, no nothing. She would just take off running like Usain Bolt, in his prime. My sister falls apart. She took piano lessons and one of my favorite things to do was to sneak up on her while she was practicing and just yell right into her ear. Some people get angry. Those people will chase you with a cast iron frying pan; that's my wife. Some people freeze. They cannot move at all, they cannot speak.

Fear does strange things to people. We all have fears. Faith is not an absence of fear. Faith is trusting God, and God is love. The greatest command is to love God and love others. There is no greater love than that we lay down our lives for another. Perfect love drives out fear. That is the truth, right out of the Word. Faith doesn't drive out fear, love does. If you want to live a life of freedom from fear, we go to the Word. As I have said before, we tend to change our thoughts to fit the truth. We keep telling ourselves the truth while it is what God says that *is* the truth. It is not my emotions, my intellect or reasoning skills, my opinions, my five senses, and it is not my experiences that are the truth. What God says is the truth. He is trustworthy. Over and over in the Word we see Him described as good, as loving and merciful, and as kind. Even when you are sitting in a Cessna drenched in your own cold sweat, trying with all your might to hear from Him, He is worthy of your trust, because He is love.

Again, God is not a teddy bear. He is not my buddy, my hombre, my bro. He is God. He is LORD. That means master, owner. He will test you to see if you are trustworthy. You can expect tests. Peter did. He denied knowing Jesus three times, but then on the day of Pentecost, less than two months later, Peter stood before all the Jews (in Acts 2) and spoke the truth. "You killed Jesus, He arose and is with Father, and now you have the opportunity to repent. And by the way, this is what Joel prophesied. Now we have the Helper, the Power, the Comforter, with us. Oh yeah, remember the pillar of fire our fathers followed? Well it is now dispersed and on the heads of many, not just the priests. It's on everyone." Wow! What changed? How did Peter change from being scared of a young girl to standing before the leaders of his people? How did Peter move from doubt and fear to the power and wisdom to speak with boldness and authority? Was it love? Jesus asked him three times, do you love me, and Peter said "yes." Just loving Him isn't enough. Just knowing you are loved is not enough. There is more. More good news. The Gospel is more than just knowing Jesus, saying a prayer when you were 10 years old. The Gospel is the gospel of the Kingdom. The good news is that we do not have to wait until the sweet by and by, just tolerating our time on earth until we get up there to the

Promised Land. This here right now is the Promised Land. This is eternal life. It has already started. It is not a future wish. You are not a scared kid. You are a son of the Living God, the Most High, the King of Kings, the Lord of Lords. And that is awesome.

Holy Spirit came. He is in us. He is with us. He empowers us. With Him we are more than conquerors; with Him we can do all things. With Him we can heal the sick, cleanse the lepers and cast out demons. With Him we can love well. With Him we can expand our hearts to love more. We can begin to see through His eyes. With Him we can hear directly from Him because He talks to us. With Him we can change our thought patterns to think like Him. He came to show us that love looks like something. As John Wimber said, "We all get to play." The only way you are left out is if you choose not to play.

THE BENEFITS OF SONSHIP

We can learn a lot from past generations. People like my grandparents, who lived through a world war, learned to be content in their "today." They learned to take on the responsibilities they were given with determination and grit. They fought for freedom, living without entitlement. They lived in a place few of us in the West have had to live. Not knowing what tomorrow would bring, they loved well in the moment and held loosely to their possessions, living to love their neighbors because they understood their current conditions were not their forever story. The joy of each new morning was their "happily ever after." Sounds like Psalms and Proverbs doesn't it, like the early Church in Acts, like the Kingdom of God. It sounds like sonship.

Micah 6:8 says, *"He has shown you, O man, what is good; and what does the LORD require of you but to do justly, to love mercy, and to walk humbly with your God?"* This kind of living comes at a price. We don't just turn around one day flowing with loving kindness, humility and a heart's desire for Kingdom justice. More often than not, God has to speak to us just to get our attention about these things. You may be surprised by how He chooses to speak to you. If God could speak through a donkey, maybe just maybe He can speak through your spouse or your children. When He speaks, we need to be able to listen with humility, turn over what is said and then make adjustments. That means no more excuses when it comes to issues of pride. Pride can take us to a place where we compare ourselves to others and we keep chasing perfection in order to be the best. Pride can disguise our need for other people and keep us self-reliant. Pride can keep you from being able to receive, skewing your perspective of the Father. Pride can tell us we do not need this "religious stuff," that we are good just as we are. I'm among the first to say that we do not need religious stuff. We need the One whose name is on the front door. Too often it seems we have lost Jesus Christ in a religion that carries His name. I see people who have come out of Lo-debar and still remember the stench with a greater understanding of Christ than those who have followed religion and grown apathetic and cold. I think that Holy Spirit is busy reintroducing Christians to Christ once again because we need a reintroduction.

One way to limit God is to be our own enemy, a stubborn mule who chooses excuses over change, believing that change is not possible. I want to live my life in obedience. God is my goal.

I don't want to limit Him by my thoughts, or misconceptions, or pride. I want to build on His truths. I want to stop making excuses. We have a Papa who calls Himself "Love." Each one of us has been bought with a love gift of blood so that we can be free. We have Holy Spirit in inside of us, with us at all times. It is time to come to the family Table, to receive the benefits of being in the family. What is available to us at the Table is for our benefit, the benefit of our family, our marriage, and our friendships. It is for the benefit of our city, our nation and all the nations of the world. We get to live with the benefits of sonship.

TRUST HIM

When I was in seminary, Dr. Smith told me a story about a twelve-year-old boy who wanted to know God. It has been a while since I heard it but I remember it this way. This young fellow was so intent on his quest that he went from hut to hut in his African village trying to find someone who could help him find God. After knocking on doors one day, he met a man who said, "I can't help you, but I know someone who can. Up that path is a sage who lives up in the hills. He can help you."

The young boy immediately started the long journey up that path. After walking uphill for hours, he came to the sage's hut and knocked on the door. He was exhausted from his walk but desperate to find the answer to his question on how to find God. The door opened slowly, and a short old man with a long beard walked out. The man looked to be a 100 years old, but the boy was undeterred. He blurted out, "I want to know God."

The old man stared at him in silence and then motioned for the young fellow to follow him. The boy followed the sage to a pond. Still silent, the old man motioned for the boy to look closely into the water. As soon as the youngster's head was bent down, the sage grabbed the back of his neck and pushed his head under the water. The boy started kicking and shaking in an effort to loose himself from the grip of the sage. He feared that he had walked all that way just to be killed by some old lunatic! Just as the boy was losing strength, the sage pulled him out of the water. They sat at the water's edge for a couple of minutes, the youth staring at the sage, still gasping for breath. Finally the sage broke his silence and said sternly, "When you want God as much as you just wanted your next breath," he said, "you will find Him."

God did not change for me in that season; I changed. I stayed so single-minded about learning to trust Him that nothing else—not even my next breath—mattered. I could not get into the Word enough. I spent more time in prayer during that time than I had in the previous five years. I went after the King and the Kingdom as hard as I could and my faith grew.

Many of us struggle to understand this thing we call faith. Just what is faith, or what is it not? Faith is not ignoring the natural realm. Faith is not denial. Faith is simply saying "Yes, the natural I'm living in is real, but there's a reality that trumps this." Jesus constantly preached the reality of the Kingdom of God. He put this reality front and center in the Lord's prayer: *"Our Father which art in heaven, hallowed be thy name. Thy kingdom come...."* He actually brought the Kingdom to earth with Him, announcing its arrival. (See Mark 1:15.) We are literally living in the Kingdom of God. This Kingdom exists all around us, but until you have eyes to see, you will never walk in it. My desperate desire led me to the gospels, and the gospels lead me to Jesus. Jesus led me to the Father, and that is where I have been ever since. When you find the Father, you find everything.

CHAPTER SIX

BREAKDOWN

When my seminary studies came to a close, Wendy and I, along with two close friends, heard God calling the four of us to move to my hometown of Spartanburg, South Carolina, and start a ministry to young adults called Wayfarer. I had read a book called *Notes from a Wayfarer* written by Helmut Thielicke, a German theologian. The story of this man's life was greatly inspiring and had a powerful impact on us as young leaders. Our hero in seminary was Dr. Robert Smith Jr., and he introduced us to Thielicke at a pivotal point in our story together. In the meantime, I had told God that I would move anywhere in the world to do His ministry—anywhere but Spartanburg. I used to tell my wife that I would move to a port-a-potty, but I was not going back home. I wanted to stretch my wings and live in a place where I would not be known to so many people as Little Chad.

But God is God, and I am not. So we packed our bags and took off for Spartanburg. Through Wayfarer, we focused on preaching, teaching, and writing curriculum to help young adults want to follow Jesus Christ with all of their hearts. We did this by coming alongside churches and providing them with resources that could help their congregations grow in Jesus. We also traveled quite a bit speaking at camps, conferences, and different churches.

Our weekly worship service, called Engage, proved to be a valuable asset for many young people. I cut my teeth as I learned to minister to those in the midst of the difficult twenty-something life phase. Wayfarer put on Engage for young adults from all over upstate South Carolina. We watched as Jesus used the services as a catalyst to help these individuals figure out how to follow Him. Even now, about once a month, I run into someone who was deeply affected by Engage.

During this era of my life, I decided that, since I was getting older and Wendy and I were expecting our first child, I should come off of all medication for anxiety and depression. I loved ministering to people and sharing the message of God with them, and, honestly, I was no longer in counseling and was weary of being on medication. It seemed to be a great idea—but my follow-through was all wrong. I learned the hard way that life has a way of getting bumpy when you take matters into your own hands.

I decided to stop taking the Zoloft and Klonopin, but I (foolishly) did not check with my doctor. Some medications have powerful effects on the body, and that generally includes medications for anxiety and depression. I had no idea that you pay a big price for coming off of medications like those cold turkey. Today there are organizations like Point of Return in Westlake Village, California, that help people come off of medications without sending their central nervous systems into shock. I know that now, and I wish I had known that then. I tapered off way too fast after being on those medications for twelve years. My body rebelled, hard. My head hurt so badly I did not want to open my eyes. I had a burning sensation and tingling in my brain. I felt foggy, and my neck hurt. Some days seemed like an eternity.

Things got so bad that I began to journal. I am not proud to admit that I hate journaling although I want to be a good "journaler." I wish I could be cool and head to Starbucks with a leather journal, a fancy pen, skinny jeans and a $30 coffee mug. But I have none of those things. If I tried to put on a pair of Diesels, I would throw my back out. Yet in this season of pain, I was journaling more than Henri Nouwen. Many times, the only thing I could do to get through the day was to write down my thoughts.

Have you ever been there? Have you ever had something happen to you that makes the clock seem stuck? I remember staring at the clock many days wishing night would hurry up and come so that I could get into bed and lie there. I cannot tell you how many sleepless nights I endured. And when I did sleep, I had dreams of me in my casket, people trying to kill me and storms coming at me. I kept functioning and ministering, but the days were long and hard.

And then it happened. At 28 years old, I was in the single worst moment of my life, curled up in a fetal position on my kitchen floor. I could hear my wife in the other room talking to my brother, asking him what to do. I was out of hope and

Wendy was out of hope. There comes a moment where you wonder if God is even real at all, much less if He wants to bless you. This was my moment. The seminary degree that hung on my wall meant nothing to me as I lay there on the floor crying my eyes out. I was having a nervous breakdown, detoxing from powerful chemicals from medicine. I had been trying to make sense of why I was having so many demonic dreams at night, while also suffering from pure exhaustion. I did not want to live and I did not want to die. The only word I can use to describe that season of my life was *hell*. I was going through *hell*.

Lying prone on the floor, I thought, "I just can't do this anymore." I seriously thought I was about to lose my marriage, my mind, my job. And, for the first time in my life I thought I was going to lose my faith too. I had zero belief that I would ever get through the hell I was experiencing. I later read how Henri Nouwen classified these times as the "dark night of the soul." Unless you have been there, it is difficult to understand. In these dark nights, you doubt the very existence of God Himself. You go to places you aren't sure you can survive. I felt like Jacob must have felt toward the end of his wrestling match with God. Even more, I felt like Job when he cursed even the day he was born. (See Job 3:1.) The same person who had gotten me through so much on this earth in my past now seemed non-existent. I was at the end of myself. I did not know what to do.

During this season, I still had to preach to make a living. I didn't want to preach to please God, or even to help people. If anyone listening knew what was in my heart, they would have walked out of the building. I even preached through the book of Job with a team at a Bible Study, but that made my hell more real because I was focused on how this man in Scripture questioned his very existence. There's a saying that your biggest breakthroughs are preceded by your biggest breakdowns. This was certainly my biggest breakdown. One night, as I lay there trying not to sleep, I began to pray quietly. "God," I said, "If You even care or if You are even there, help. I give up." This prayer wasn't coming from someone who had not seen God as real. I had seen God do many things before. It was just that in the middle of my hell, my wrestling match, I did not care about the past. I doubted what I had seen. I doubted who He was. I doubted everything.

My problems were not just physical and emotional. True, I was battling sickness from chemical detoxification, but I was also going through a season of spiritual warfare. You might wonder how I could make a distinction between withdrawal and warfare, considering the wrenching bodily effects of going off certain medications. I can only say that I was learning more about the spiritual realm, and that included the enemy's attacks.

Among other nightmares, I could sense that our house had a dark presence in it. I walked around praying and anointing doorposts, pictures, TVs, and our furniture with oil, committing our lives to the Lord again and again. If you come to our house today, you will find a picture on which you can still see where I put a heavy dose of oil. I figured that I would just "tough out" the cold turkey withdrawal, since I had come this far, but the spiritual battle seemed to have no answers. I did not know of a single church that I could go to for help. Can you imagine walking up to a pastor and saying, "Pastor, a presence of evil is living in our house. Could you come take a look?" Me, either.

But then something happened for Wendy and me that changed everything. In a random encounter at an event at which I was speaking, I met a woman who gave me her dad's business card. He was a counselor and he understood spiritual attacks. Wendy and I decided it was time to get help so we got in the car and drove nine hours to this man's office. Desperation, as I said earlier, does not seem to move God, but it sure will move a person. And when you move quickly toward Him, you seem to find Him more quickly.

FACE TO FACE

When Wendy and I arrived at the counselor's office, I didn't know what to expect. The counselor was calm, cordial and incredibly wise. A couple of hours into our session, he prayed for me. That's when *it* happened. Jesus appeared to me, Chad Norris, a born and bred Southern Baptist, in a literal open vision. He walked right up to me and said, "I'm your healer. Trust me." He said it twice. Love flowed through me like liquid as I stared right at Jesus. I don't know what heaven is going to be like, but if it's anything like my experience with the King of the universe, I can't wait. The One who created it all held me. The One who walked on this earth with His disciples and flipped the world upside down was with me. I'm still not over it all of these years later. I pray I never get over it.

What happened to me was not an impression or a mental image; I was *seeing* Him. I had never heard of anything like this

72

before. Jesus was about 5-foot-11 and 180 pounds. He had light brown hair, a light beard and wore a white tunic. Angels stood on either side of Him. One of them had a huge sword, and the other did not.

From the time I was a child I had heard stories about this man named Jesus. I went to Vacation Bible School as a little boy and listened to the teachers' descriptions of Him. My grandmother would talk about Him, and to Him, and would tell me dramatic scenes from the New Testament. My little mind was filled with wonder: *I wish I could walk on water,* I thought. He fascinated me all of my life. And here I was looking at Him. As He looked at me, His eyes pierced through me with violent gentleness. It was overpowering. It is a waste of time to try to describe what His love was like. I simply cannot. But what I am telling you is true: I saw Jesus that day. If you want to chuck this book into the trash, I understand. I have always been skeptical when people write about things like this. Yet, it happened.

What separated this experience from the one I had had a few years earlier in my dorm room in Campbellsville was that in Campbellsville I did not see anything. In that instance, I was overwhelmed by the glory of almighty God. But this time, it was like watching a movie—except it was more real than that. I was *in* the movie. I honestly have no idea what to call it. Some use the term *open vision.* The one thing I know is that everything changed for me in that moment. And it was not only that I saw Him: Jesus came to me and held me close. I have never felt love like that in my life. I hit the floor. My wife, alarmed, asked, "What happened?" It was a while before I could speak.

If at this point you think I was crazy, I understand. I thought I was crazy, too. But it happened. I have been reluctant to talk about that day too much because I thought that people would find it hard to believe. I never want to come across as an idiot. So I decided it was best to keep my mouth shut about the encounter. I was not at a worship service. I was not caught up in some glory cloud. I was a conservative type of guy with a health problem. I was a Baptist to the core who secretly never wanted to walk out on the waters of anything that would draw attention. Yet in that one moment, everything changed for me.

I cannot tell you how many times I prayed to Jesus: "Wreck me with who You are. I want all of You. Show me who You are." I know I never expected Jesus to answer those prayers of mine like He did. Jesus Christ of Nazareth walked up to me in an open vision. That was way out of my comprehension. I had no paradigm for it. I wonder how our biblical heroes felt when weird stuff happened to them. Can you imagine being Cornelius and having an angel walk up to you and say, "Hey, how's it going? God likes you and your offerings" (see Acts 10:1-6). Thomas did not have a vision of Jesus; the resurrected Jesus came strolling in as though He was looking for something to eat and said, "Thomas, go ahead and touch My hands and My side" (see John 20:27). The Bible offers an extensive list of people who had interactions with God. We love to talk about those people, but we often have a hard time comprehending it when it happens to us.

We seem to listen more carefully to pastors and leaders who are really smart and can give the dimensions of the boat Noah built. I understand that. People have fabricated stories of signs and wonders over the years, abusing what some call charismatic things. But we cannot use that as an excuse to hide behind a false pretense of who Jesus is and what Jesus is like. People who fight against "experiences" with God so furiously generally fear experiencing Him. It is possible to memorize the book of Galatians and not know the God of the Bible. Rather than consider those encounters as "weird," it should be weirder to follow a supernatural God and never experience the supernatural. If my life is not super*natural* to some degree, then it is super*ficial* to a great degree.

I have heard many times, "Don't be so heavenly minded that you are no earthly good." It might be truer that we are so earthly minded that heaven has a hard time doing much good through us. I have been asking the Lord to get me to a place in my life where I can live consistently with one ear there and one here. In Roger's office that day, I discovered that that is the only way I want to live.

When I saw the Lord, His love knocked me out of my chair. It was not a handshake love. It was a messy, wild, passionate, deep, perfect love. It was the kind of love that makes you not care what anyone else in the world thinks about you. Because of that experience, I can see why the early Christians laughed as Nero burned them at the stake. They had such revelation of the love of God that they did not care even about death. When I say I felt love, it is an understatement. All I could say to Wendy, when I could speak, was, "He is so full of love."

Years later I can still picture Him the way He looked that day. As I mentioned, I have told this story only rarely. One time I tried to tell about it at a conference. The conference was great, people were connecting with me, and Jesus was doing some wonderful ministry. But when I shared this story—*bam!* It was like hitting a brick wall. My encounter with Jesus went over like a pregnant pole vaulter—that is to say, not well. Recently, I was talking about these events from the stage of our church, including the warfare details, and a man got up and took his three kids out of the service. He will probably never come back to our church.

Maybe part of the reason that stories like this are hard to comprehend is that so many individuals have been manipulated in the name of Jesus. Perhaps it is also because people know Jesus from a historical standpoint rather than as a present-tense Savior. The early disciples did a lot of ministry in the supernatural, and they did not even have a New Testament. We have ten Bibles in every house, and yet we get nervous when unusual things happen—even when those things parallel the stories we find in those Bibles. Instead, we should recognize when Jesus shows up in our lives in supernatural ways. After all, He did say, *"My sheep listen to my voice"* (John 10:27 NIV).

THROUGH THE EYE OF THE NEEDLE

A couple of nights after my encounter with Jesus Christ, I told Him out loud, "Show me everything. I want to know You. I want to know You and God the Father so well that I don't know where I begin and where You end. I want intimacy with You. I want such deep friendship with You that I smell like You. I'm Yours." I told the Holy Spirit that I surrendered to Him and His power to the best of my ability.

When you get to the point in your life that you are tired of flirting with Jesus and the Kingdom and you are ready to give yourself to Him, He will see to it that you have a catalyst moment. After that vision, I was "all in." Looking back on it all these years later, I can say that this process has been gentler and calmer than I was expecting. Perhaps you do not have to be obnoxious to walk in the ways of heaven after all. I still think about how natural Jesus was when I saw Him. He simply told me that He loved me.

Wendy knew something had happened to me. I knew in that moment that I had a major problem on my hands—because the God I went to seminary to learn about was not the same God I met that day. It's hard to explain. That one encounter created a hunger in me that has not decreased to this day 15 years later. I knew enough theologically to understand that the Son and the Father were the same, (see Heb. 1:3) and in that moment, I knew I had been tricked by the enemy. The misconception was revealed—the Father had to be just as loving as the Savior I had just experienced. satan was unmasked.

When Wendy and I left the counselor's office, I made a plea to God. It went like this: "I'm begging You to show me who You are. I'll follow You no matter what. I don't care what happens to my life. I must know You even if it costs me everything." Starting the night, when I prayed that prayer, my misconceptions started to transform into correct conceptions of who God is, what His nature is, and how He sees me. The revelation that Our Father loves us and wants to bless us, that He wants us to have a close relationship with Him and to walk in truth, became real to me, and has remained real to me ever since. I know that I belong, that I have a home with the Father. It's so important to know that we belong. This knowing, this belonging is part of our true identity.

It was after this experience that I decided to do something I had never done before—really read the gospels. I had learned at Beeson that the first chapter of Hebrews paints a picture of Jesus and His Father as being identical. If that was true—and I believed it to be—then something was wrong with my view. I had never felt love such as I felt with Jesus, and, according to the Word, that is the way His Dad is, too. I wanted to know more. I think this is what Paul talked about in Ephesians 3:14-21 when he said that he prayed for us to be filled with the full measure of God's love and then described that love.

I score as an ENFP on the Myers-Briggs Type Indicator, which translates into "Let's *go* for it." That is the way I operated in this instance. I did not jump into the gospel kiddie pool with inflatable water wings. I cannonballed into the deep end Rambo-style and swam as if my life depended upon it. I wanted to know just how much I could trust Jesus Christ and expect to see His Kingdom power at work.

For a long season, I had my head buried in the gospels so intently that I ignored my usual hobbies. Have you ever noticed that people who walk in what is perceived as "extreme faith" make those around them either incredibly tense or incredibly inspired? There seems to be no neutral ground. The more you observe the way Jesus operated in the natural realm, the more it will affect the way in which you go about your daily life. I will never forget the night Wendy said, "I just wish you would watch *SportsCenter* for a change." I never thought in a million years I would hear her say that. But as I started observing Jesus in the gospels, His Father opened my eyes to realities I had never known. The longer I stayed in the gospels, the more my grid of what it means to follow Jesus began to change.

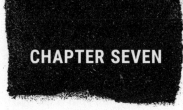
FRIENDSHIP WITH GOD

When my son Jack was three he loved to tell people, "You are my best friend." It seems as though we have something built in us by God Himself that desires to connect to others in deep friendship. We want to know and be known, to be intimate with another person in friendship. I wish I had known as a child that we long to have this kind of relationship with God as well. And that is what I want to ponder in this chapter—knowing the Father. What does it mean—not only after we die, but right now, today? Let's start with the basics. What does it mean to know, really know, someone?

INTIMACY

When I started dating Wendy, my heart was beating for more than just conversations about how her classes were going. There comes a point when a 22-year-old male wants to do more than hold his fiancee's hand. Yes, I am talking about sex. The Church has an opportunity to define sexuality in healthy ways. The Creator of the world invented it. It is fun. It is normal. It is pure. It is heaven's agenda for married couples. After being married for fifteen years, Wendy and I have learned together as a couple that God's intention for His invention is more than just a physical act though. I heard this in a marriage seminar early on, but it has taken me a while to realize that this is true.

I remember telling Wendy that we had to get married quick because I could not stay engaged to her for a long time and remain sane. It was not easy. It never is. Sometimes when you are dating someone, you feel as though you are on high alert all the time. At least, you feel this way if you are trying to honor the Lord with purity. Why is this? I believe that our Father put something inside of us that longs for connection on a deep level beyond simply talking with the love of your life. If I ever say, "Intimacy is not my thing," I may need someone to beat me in the head with a boat paddle, because something is wrong with me. Intimacy is something God created us for. When He told Adam and Eve to go and multiply, He was not talking about a board game. He basically said, "I made both of you. Go enjoy your nakedness and have fun. Be intimate."

God wants us to have intimacy. Sex is part of this in marriage, but only part. In the Father's eyes, it is not normal to have a solely cordial relationship between spouses. He wants spouses to be close, intimate. Likewise, He wants to be close to us. The first thing I tell people who want to see the Kingdom manifest is this: "Get to know God more intimately than anyone you have ever known—through His Word, soaking in His presence, music, and fellowship with other believers." If the supernatural is something that you want to become natural in your life, you simply have to understand this. I have never met anyone who walks in the Father's works who does not understand intimacy.

When we teach at our church about how to walk in the supernatural naturally, we start with intimacy. Intimacy with the Creator of the world will naturally lead to His Kingdom manifesting in our lives. When Jesus becomes the lover of our souls, extending His Kingdom is not something that we have to strive to do. When we want Him more than we want anything else in the world, we will see His works flow naturally from our walk with Him. He is not asking us to memorize powerful prayers. He is asking us to draw close to Him and then closer still. Jesus demonstrated this by the way He always sought seclusion from the crowds in order to be with His Father. As He did, He grew in wisdom and favor (see Luke 2:52). So can we.

There is much to be discovered about the implications of walking in intimacy with God. Jesus told the God-fearing people around Him, *"You do not know me or my Father"* (John 8:19 NIV). The longer Peter lived, the more he became acquainted with the God who sent His Son, and with Jesus, the Son—a man whom Peter walked with. Peter transitioned from a self-consumed, impulsive, fearful follower to someone whose shadow made others whole. Ministering in authority is not about being cocky, it is about exercising God's power. The authority to do so is cultivated through deep and consistent intimacy with Him. Jesus is our perfect example of what it looks like when one person is completely abandoned to this idea of intimacy with God Almighty.

Jeremiah said that if we boast about anything we should boast that we know God. This fiery prophet gives us a sneak peek into what Jesus talked about in the following passage, yet it takes some digging to understand what Jeremiah is talking about here.

> *This is what the Lord says: "Let not the wise boast of their wisdom or the strong boast of their strength or the rich boast of their riches, but let the one who boasts boast about this: that they have the understanding to know me, that I am the Lord, who exercises kindness, justice and righteousness on earth, for in these I delight," declares the Lord* (Jeremiah 9:23-24 NIV).

KNOWING AND BEING KNOWN BY GOD

One day while studying in my office at work, I decided to track down the meaning of the word that my Bible translated as "know." What did Jeremiah mean by "knowing" God? The answer for me was the Hebrew word *yada*. The only time I had ever heard *yada* was when I would hear someone say, "Yada, Yada, Yada," to describe someone else who would not shut up. But learning the Hebrew meaning made me feel as if I had gone through that little rabbit hole in *Alice in Wonderland*. Eight years later, I am still searching for the fullness of this little word. I cannot tell you how many times in seminary I said, "I would rather be attacked by a wild llama than be in this Hebrew class." I hated studying Hebrew. For one thing, I was terrible at it. Where other people saw letters formed in the lines and curves on their pages, I seemed to be staring at one gigantic, chaotic mess. So it is funny that God took one teeny-weeny little Hebrew word and used it to flip my world upside down.

In Hebrew, *yada* is not just about head knowledge of God. It describes intimate connection to Him. This same Hebrew word is used in Genesis 4:1, which says that *"Adam knew Eve his wife; and she conceived"* (KJV). Let that sink in for a second. A child is conceived when man is with woman in the most intimate act; when he "knows" her. So what in the world was Jeremiah talking about here when he said we should know God? Obviously he was not being gross or indecent. Instead, God is telling us through His prophet that He loves it when we walk in close intimacy with Him.

As I began my study of *yada*, I literally said out loud: "God, let me get this straight—I can talk to You as a man talks to his friend? I can seriously talk to You and learn to hear Your voice and know You closely?" God said yes. At first I wondered how I would distinguish God's voice from mine. I thought the whole thing was crazy. Yet the further I went down the rabbit hole, the more I realized that there was a Kingdom life that I knew nothing about and it involved talking with God.

By studying this word, I got revelation that this God, who I thought was mad at me, actually wanted to walk in intimacy with me. *Yada* opened my eyes to the possibility that there was a deeper expression of experiential intimacy with God and I wanted to explore it fully. One thing I discovered as I explored is that extreme intimacy with the Father makes the enemy incredibly nervous—even terrified. Mind you, I spend very little time thinking about what the enemy is up to. My goal is to get as close to the Father as possible. Building a deep friendship with God is the ultimate pursuit. This got me to thinking about the idea that sheep like me really have only one job. They need to stay close to the shepherd and keep their eyes on him. Closeness brings intimacy.

Perhaps God is closer than you think. Perhaps He enjoys being part of even the small details of your life. One day during this time, I was writing a check for our monthly mortgage payment and I heard, *Don't write that*. Somehow I knew it was God speaking to me, but I wrote the check anyway only to realize a week later that Wendy had already written one. I know that many people who are very serious about God will reject what I have just written because it seems small and childish. But I think that being childish might lead us to a world we would never otherwise consider. God is inviting us into an intimate relationship with Him as His children. What an incredible invitation. Why is it so hard to understand? My beloved Mama Jane was the one who brought me to the intersection of my little world and God's big heart.

GOD IS NOW MY FATHER

My grandmother who I affectionately refer to as Mama Jane used to take me fishing when I was a kid. Even now, I can close my eyes and smell the Georgia air as it came across my uncle Jack's pond. We never fished for bass because Mama Jane always wanted to fish for bream. I put live crickets on my hook and tossed my line out into the calm waters. Those times felt like perfection to me. It was not the water. It was not how the fish

86

were biting. It was my grandmother. She actually talked to me and asked me how I was doing and what I wanted for dinner that night. She listened to me and gave me advice on how to fish well. It was just the two of us sitting in the same boat enjoying each other. Sometimes I sat in her lap. It is possible that woman never fully realized what happened inside my heart when she held me. I felt connected to her. It would take me years to figure out that my relationship with Mama Jane was a taste of what is available to me with the God of the universe. It happened one afternoon in Haiti. God said to me, *"You still don't know how kind I am. Why is it so easy for you to think of the kindness of Mama Jane, but you still have a hard time thinking of Me as kind?"* God used something in the natural to teach me about the spiritual (see John 3:12).

Have you noticed that Jesus called God "Father" most of the time? Almost always—until He got to the cross. The religious establishment got incredibly aggravated when Jesus talked about His Father. (See John 8, for example.) If you think charismatic things make people feel uncomfortable, try telling them that you are intimate with the Maker of heaven and earth. People didn't like it when Jesus did it, and many don't like it when they hear it from someone now. Yet, more and more, all over the world, people are becoming intimate with the Father. Things that used to be considered charismatic are becoming normal. That is because the supernatural is not about putting on a show—or even about expressing a belief system. It comes from a deep intimate connection between a person and God. People ask me all the time if I am charismatic. I used to respond by asking, "What do you mean by that statement?" These days

I answer by saying, "God is now my Father, and I like Him a lot. That is what I am."

Recently I went to a conference with more than ten thousand people in attendance. The speakers, who are well-known preachers and teachers, used the word *Father* only once or twice during the whole conference. It seems odd to me that we follow God's Son but hardly ever refer to God the way Jesus did. Jesus' vocabulary was full of the word *Father*; that is how Jesus knew Him. Do you refer to God as "Father"? If not, open a door in your heart and ask Him to show you why not. I think that part of the reason so many people do not call God "Father" is that they had pathetic examples in their own fathers. As a result, it is difficult for them to consider that God could be different from what they have seen modeled, and they are not eager to replicate that experience.

Calling God "Father" instead of "God" may seem like a small difference, but in reality it is as wide as an ocean. You can tell a lot about a person by how he or she refers to God. As I have said, Jesus referred to God as His Father, and called His miracles the works of His Father. Jesus operated with power, and it flowed out of this intimate connection. But as stirring as that was, maybe the most stunning thing Jesus said was to call God "Abba." I want to show you why this was such a bombshell to His listeners.

OUR APPROACHABLE GOD

It would be as awkward for Andrew and Thomas to call God "Daddy" as it would be for you to go grocery shopping naked. But this miracle-working carpenter's Son, this unlikely rabbi, talked about calling the thundering God of the world "Daddy."

I think many of us have been taught to turn God's image into something we can be comfortable with and manage well. I can promise you one thing: I never once thought of calling God "Daddy" when I was younger. One time in my youth group a girl called Him "Daddy" in a prayer, and we all laughed at her. Several of us even tried to get her to move to the crazy church down the street where she would fit in better. Little did I know that she understood something that would take me years to discover. So I can relate to Andrew, Thomas, Luke, and those others who would have looked at Jesus as though He were a crazy person.

Put yourself in their shoes. The disciples were so stinking real that it is not even funny. They had front-row seats to the most astonishing story of all time, and they were basically clueless. They make me feel better about my own cluelessness. Of the many head-scratching times the disciples experienced during their three years with Jesus, the one that stands out to me as probably most challenging for them was Jesus' revelation about God. Their baseline about God, taken from centuries—millennia—of careful religious training, established Him as unapproachable. They knew all the Bible stories of God's refusal to compromise. (We have already noted how Aaron's two sons brought "unholy fire" to the altar of sacrifice and got smoked.) God told His people, recorded in Exodus 19:22, that if the priests did not consecrate themselves, they would get it, too. God just did not seem very nice. His holiness was uncomfortable.

Nor did He seem approachable. Moses wanted badly to see God (see Exod. 33:18-23), but God said that Moses could view only His back as He passed by. When you think of God in the Old Testament, the chances of connecting with Him intimately seem remote. So when Jesus called God "Abba," we can imagine Peter saying something like, "Jesus, let me get this straight. What I hear you saying is that you are God's Son. Even though you grew up in a very average town that never produces anything good, and even though your parents are Mary and Joseph, you are telling me that from now on, you want me to get to know your Father—who is God—as my Father, and call Him *Abba*?"

When is the last time you called God "Daddy"? Let's take it one step further and use the word *Da-da*. The word *Abba* in Aramaic is extremely intimate in the way *Da-da* is. Even now, if you go to Jerusalem you will hear little children saying "Abba, Abba" as they talk to their dads.

THE UNFATHOMABLE LOVE OF THE FATHER

Sam, Ruthie and Jack are three children with three different personalities, but they share one major theme: As their daddy, I would do anything for them to bless their lives. These three amazing little people have a couple of similarities and a ton of differences. Sam is our "old soul." When he was nine, he was the type to sit on the front porch and talk about the good ol' days. He is tenderhearted, loyal, and responsible. As the big brother he has always helped raise his sister and brother. Sam traveled with me a lot when he was little and has been a good companion, a friend. As he grows into a man and walks through challenge and conflict, even with me, I have watched his heart stay tender and grow strong at the same time. He's the one I can say

90

nothing to for hours in the car and it'll have been the best part of our day.

Ruthie is my passionate one. She's stubborn, zealous, and determined, yet she is sweet, adorable, and thoughtful. She wants to know where the boundaries are. She may or may not cross them, but she always wants to know exactly where they are so that she can decide. She is the one that I can be laughing with one second and crying with the next. I see Jesus in Ruthie's eyes. I have noticed this more and more and I think she teaches me more about Him than I do her. I love how Ruthie brings excitement to our house. She has never had a boring day.

Jack is one of a kind. I probably have never met anyone like Jack. He is funny, gregarious and wild to the core. When he was little it was no big deal to walk into the bathroom and find Jack attempting a handstand with his head in the commode. Whereas Ruthie will test the boundaries, Jack knows no boundaries. One day at a golf course, I decided to let him walk as far as he would go simply to see where he ended up. He got 150 yards away from me before he finally turned around. He loves to wrestle, eat Cheetos and hit stuff. We call him Jack-Jack because his personality is so big he deserves to have his name said twice. He is the one who had the biggest potential to send me back on medication.

The grace of Jesus has a hard time flowing in our lives when we fail to understand how much God our Father loves us. As I said, as a dad I would do anything for my children, and that is exactly the way our heavenly Father feels about us. This truth has changed everything for me. When we can grasp this concept, we will live holier lives by accident than we ever could by trying without that revelation. From the very beginning, God has always wanted the best for His people. Look back to Genesis 12:1-3 and see for yourself. It is impossible to describe what is in my heart toward my children. I love them. How do you describe love? There are no words. All I know is that a father's love is real and deep. Jesus is an exact representation of His Father, who loves us with an unfathomable love. It is too good to be true and yet it is.

It is not just a theological exercise to think thoughts like this. If you do not have a deep revelation of how kind God is, you will find it nearly impossible to see major breakthroughs when you pray for people. If you are where I was and you are tired of not seeing the Kingdom manifest in your life more, start focusing your mind on His kindness, forgiveness and unconditional love. Then start praying for people.

FRIENDSHIP IS THE GOAL

When my kids were young, the scene was almost always the same when I would come home from work. The boys would be going about their business. Sam watching TV or doing homework and Jack probably tearing up something. Ruthie, however, would be locked and loaded and ready for assault. Whether I had been gone for five minutes or five days, when I would walk through that door, she would run straight at me and scream "Daddy!" She would jump up into my arms and squeeze me tight. I have equally strong connections with Sam and Jack, but my connection with Ruthie is different. Not better; just different. It touches a special place in my heart. Pulling into the driveway I would anticipate my baby girl running right at me. Once while I was shopping with Ruthie she looked up at me and said, "I love you, Daddy." I wanted to sit down and cry. I never get tired of hearing that.

But every once in a while, when I would come home, Ruthie would be nowhere in sight. And when she was not bounding toward me, I noticed. I missed it. That is because I love it when one of my children calls me "Daddy." Sam does not call me "Daddy"; he calls me "Dad." Jack usually grunts at me. But not Ruthie. My girl calls me "Daddy."

Now, if I phoned my own father right now and called him "Daddy," he would ask me if I were okay. To be honest with you, he would probably think that I was on something. A grown man typically does not call his father "Daddy"; it sounds so intimate. And that probably explains why you hardly ever hear anyone call God "Father," much less "Abba" or "Daddy." I believe God gets a ton of glory when one of His children refers to Him with the term He told Jesus to tell us to call Him. The disciples struggled with this concept, but Paul seemed to have a better revelation about it. Paul used the word *Abba* in Galatians 4:6. Paul was not someone you would call a "feeler." As a matter of fact, Paul lived as one of the most driven, unfeeling personalities I have ever read about. Yet after he met Jesus, he joined in teaching us to relate to God as Daddy.

Right now I have a man crush on Paul. I never really paid that much attention to him compared to my obsession with Simon Peter and John. Those two usually claim most of my attention for whatever reason. But right now, Paul fascinates me. Paul, an extremist, protected the Jewish lifestyle, and he killed Christians to do it. He was a big deal. Then one day out of nowhere, Jesus knocked him down and everything changed. Paul stopped denying Jesus and began preaching Jesus' message about Abba. He even raised the dead on the side. Paul *got it*. He understood that trying to walk in the power of God without knowing Abba is useless striving. It produces tones that are no more melodic than a clanging gong.

Most people fear that walking in intimacy with Abba means being embarrassingly emotional. But remember, Paul told us that the Kingdom of God is not a matter of talk but of power. In other words, we cannot live in power without a revelation of Abba. If we want more of His power working in our lives, we do not need to focus on faith; we need to focus on intimacy with the Creator of the world. As I have said, we have more problems with love and intimacy than we have with faith. Faith operates by love (see Gal. 5:6). If I never refer to God as "Father," "Abba" or "Daddy," then I need to seriously evaluate whether I have gotten to know God through His Word or through other sources.

Some years back, I was concerned about what others thought of me when I talked about things like this. I would seek Abba in the privacy of my own home, but I would really tone down my language in public. It was a little embarrassing to call Him "Daddy" in front of others—and I wanted their affirmation. The fear of man is a powerful motivator. Finally, I got to the point where I did not care anymore. If Jesus called Him "Father" or "Abba," then I was going to pursue Him in the same way. As I got to know my Abba, I started to see Him do some incredible things.

I recently listened to a very popular preacher and the whole time he was preaching I thought, *He is presenting God as one of the most miserable people I have ever heard of.* Would someone who intimately knows God present Him in such a negative way? Paul was not vague about this. He burned for one thing: to know Father, Son and Holy Spirit as intimately as possible. Check out what Paul said at the end of his life: "I want to know Christ and the power of His resurrection" (see Phil. 3:10). This word *know* suggests deep, intimate, experiential connection with someone. It sounds a lot like *yada* in Hebrew.

When Jesus came to earth, He reconnected His followers with the idea of God's desire to walk closely with His people. Let that sink in. God sent Jesus here and then chose to reside inside of His people. He wants to be close to us. He wants a deep abiding friendship with you and me that starts on this earth and takes us in to eternity. Adam and Eve walked intimately with God from the very beginning, until satan got into the mix and broke that intimacy. Jesus came and restored the intimate connection between the Father and His children—you and me. Friendship with God is not only possible. It is the goal. All else pales in comparison. God intends that the supernatural lifestyle that flows from intimacy with Him be normal in the life of every believer. Are you hungry for God's normal? For intimacy with the One who created you and all things? I am.

CHAPTER EIGHT

SELFLESSLY TAKING UP YOUR CROSS

God undeniably put my wife and I together. We both knew it soon after that first awkward kiss. As we started dating, we began heading toward a lifetime of pursuing God and serving Him together. When you are young and in love, as we were, you have zero concept of what awaits you on the other side of "I do." The other side is a daily reminder that you are not the most important person in the world, and that the goal of marriage is to out-give, out-forgive, and out-serve the other person. Little did either of us know in the moments after that awkward first kiss how hard it would be to learn selflessness and discover what taking up our cross in our marriage actually looks like.

I have heard about the 3, 7, or 15-year itch to move on from marriage. I have no idea if any of these numbers are true, but it's interesting how many times I hear this as I pastor people. I just never thought I would be itchy. I never thought in a million years that divorce would be an option for Wendy and me.

When I said, "I do," I meant it. I am a loyal person by nature, and I hadn't had a single thought of our marriage not lasting before "it" hit. "It" was another dark night of the soul, another season that literally stretched our faith to the brink of giving up. Our marriage hit this place, and neither one of us saw it coming. There were no affairs, pornography addictions, financial crises, or any other major event that tears so many marriages apart. We simply got to the place where we could not be in the same room together very long without disagreeing or arguing about something. I remember sitting in my recliner one night and thinking, "There is a realistic chance of me going through what I never thought was an option." It was a scary place that left us both feeling hopeless. There appeared to be no resolution in sight to the continuous conflict. Life got scarier as the arguments become calmer, as if we had both resigned ourselves to the fact that it would never get better. When that kind of apathy sets in, the enemy goes to work.

One night, I walked outside and took a baseball bat to my trash can. I pounded on that trash can as I wept. I've heard it said many times that our biggest breakthroughs come after our biggest breakdowns. In that moment, I highly doubted it. If you had asked either one of us about the cause of this inability to get along, I'm not sure we would have been able to articulate it. There is no telling how much warfare we go through as we give our lives to Jesus and His Kingdom. All we knew is that we needed help. We had reached the point in life where we knew we had better do something drastic or things would never change. We had to risk vulnerability in order to see change. For Zacchaeus, that moment came at the foot of a fig tree. Our fig tree was in Buena Vista, Colorado, at Crossroads Christian Counseling. As pastors, we knew it was risky to let our guard down and admit we needed help. After I weighed the cost, I decided I did not care what others thought. We needed help, and it was time to let our guards down. Without vulnerability, there was little chance of breakthrough for us.

My wife and I sat down and talked one night about the reality of our situation. There was no yelling or hatred. We were both simply scared, fragile, and numb. Wendy and I are both passionate people who fully engage the things we are passionate about. Numb is not a word to describe either of us. But on this night, it was the perfect description. As our kids slept upstairs, we discussed the magnitude of our conflict. We decided to leave the next week for a week of therapy. We landed in Denver and drove up the interstate through a truly spectacular view. On this three-hour drive, I felt like we were in a scene from *The Lord of the Rings*. I wasn't able to stop staring at the beauty of the mountains. I had no idea that this three-hour drive would begin a three-year journey of discovering what love really is. I did not realize what God was planning for our marriage. I wish I knew then what I know now—that this trip was only the first of two major, life-changing weeks for us.

Our first week in Colorado with a therapist was enlightening, intense, refreshing, and challenging. It centered on the idea of changing thought patterns and behaviors. It's interesting how the most powerful truths always make their way back to the root of who Jesus was and what He taught. Earlier in this book, I pointed out that Jesus began His ministry with, *"Repent, for the kingdom of heaven has come near"* (Matt. 4:17 NIV). This idea of repentance is all about *metanoia*—the concept of changing thought patterns. That's what Colorado was for our marriage. God challenged us gently to change the way we thought about each other and about what love was in the first place. We knew quickly in counseling that God was bringing us closer together, but we did not realize how hard it is to change thinking patterns so that they lead to transformation. It would take us three years to truly see transformational breakthrough. I am convinced, beyond a shadow of a doubt, that two things are against most people when it comes to successfully staying at the King's Table and seeing a culture of the supernatural manifest in their families and their churches. The first is an unwillingness to be vulnerable enough to see grace explode, and the second is an unwillingness to be patient enough to be astonished.

During the three years between our two trips to Colorado, we saw some improvement, off and on, in our marriage. Like most people, we took a couple of steps forward and then a few steps back. This cycle was not all bad. There were times we truly knew God was at work. The work He was doing reached a crescendo on our second trip. I can honestly say it was the deepest and most impactful week of spiritual formation I've ever had in 45 years on this big, beautiful planet.

I want to stay at the King's Table and sit as close to my Papa as possible. I want to continue to see miracles and healings. It never gets old to me. I love seeing the power of God manifest when I pray for people. I love the fact that I pastor a church that is going after the supernatural in a very natural way. We have testimonies on a weekly basis of people seeing healings in their lives. When God restores real and genuine physical ailments, we celebrate it at The Garden Greenville. Yet, even with the command of Jesus to heal the sick, and my passion to do so, there is something much greater that I have learned and experienced—and it happened in my own marriage.

CHOOSING TO BE VULNERABLE

On our second trip to counseling in Colorado, we both thought we were going for a tune-up. We were wrong. Jesus had something greater in store for us. In our second and third sessions, we came to a point where we were simply not getting along very well. We both discussed what our own needs were for each other with the help of our therapist. Midweek, I decided to go for a workout at a CrossFit gym. At the end of my workout, out of the blue, I looked up to heaven and said, "What's the point down here? What do you want from me?" Immediately I heard, *"Greater love has no one than this, than to lay down one's life for his friends"* (John 15:13). He spoke to me so clearly that it was like He was standing right beside me. I immediately got into my car and said to the Lord, "I know what love is. I just want you to show me what it is. Make it personal. I know what it is, but what is it really?" The next song that immediately came on my XM radio was one I had not heard in a long time. It was Foreigner's "I Want to Know What Love Is." The Lord has a sense of humor.

I've had the Lord tell me many things before, in my walk with Him. I've had some wild and out-of-the-box experiences with Him. I've seen blind eyes open, a gold glory cloud manifest in a church service, food multiply, and a demon-possessed lady in Haiti dramatically delivered. I have had words of knowledge over people that I could not possibly have known. I have had dreams and revelation from heaven. I have had strategic plans come to me that are beyond my ability to create. But I'll tell you right now that none of those things can hold a fork to the powerful word spoken to me by the Word Himself in this moment. I understood love on a different level. He said, "Maybe you don't have a faith problem. Maybe you simply have a love problem." I have learned to recognize the difference between knowledge and revelation. What God spoke to me was pure revelation. My response was, "OK, I get it." The next two days in counseling felt like Jesus Christ had walked into our sessions. We got more revelation on love in two days than we had in 18 years of marriage. We realized on a gut level what being a safe place meant for each other. We also started to understand on a practical level what it looked like to love each other. Our postures began to change from "not receiving" to "giving." We genuinely began to ask what the other person needed on a daily basis. Even now with our Colorado experience behind us, we realize that this is a lifelong process of choosing to be vulnerable every single day in our marriage.

It has been a long journey for us to realize what being a safe person for each other looks like, and it has not been easy. It has taken a lot of vulnerability. The point is that our vulnerability gave grace a target to hit. We have seen grace truly transform us and the way in which we see each other. I'm not sure it is possible to build deep friendship with God without walking in vulnerability. Perhaps vulnerability is a little-talked about trait of someone who flows in a high level of the prophetic. Perhaps we have made God more charismatic than He is. Perhaps if we would learn a few key principles, that even people outside of Christ are discovering, then we would see naturally supernatural cultures manifest by accident. Our time together in Colorado was so powerful that we decided to renew our vows. The Lord worked it out perfectly. A married couple who really helped us to process all that God did there in Buena Vista performed the ceremony. The whole experience was impactful because it genuinely centered on the idea of what love really is—sacrificial, giving, non-judging, powerful love.

I am convinced that we will see more supernatural power manifest in our ministries when we embrace vulnerability and love instead of focusing most of our attention on faith. Many people who begin to see healing manifest in their lives and ministries get sidetracked and pursue those things for the wrong reasons. What if, when we prayed for people, we genuinely and deeply listened and cared about the need at hand? What if we loved? Think what it could be like if we had the courage to let vulnerability lead us in the right direction. We could lead powerful communities that walk in the works and the ways of Father, while at the same time being vulnerable about where we are in our own lives. We would see more breakthrough if we could learn to boast in our weakness and allow the grace of the most magnificent person who has ever existed to flow into the brokenness in our lives and the lives of others. It's about learning to love—not just loving Jesus but loving one another too. I believe that if we could bring love into our families, our workplace, and our communities we would see God's transformational power flow abundantly.

GOING DEEPER

As a pastor, I have noticed that we tend to place blame on someone else when things don't go well in life instead of taking responsibility for our own decisions and behaviors. In counseling sessions I will hear things like, "If my mother would have raised me different then I would not be like this. If my spouse was more sold out to God then things would be different. If I had a stronger community then these things would not be happening in my life." The moment we decide that we are responsible for our own development is the moment that our life changes. In my 20 years of pastoral ministry, I have not seen significant and lasting personal growth happen unless the person is willing to take responsibility for his or her own life. One of my favorite passages in the Bible is when Jesus asks the man who has been sick for 38 years, *"Do you want to get well?"* (John 5:6 NIV). At 28 years of age I was overcome with anxiety in a fetal position on the floor. A year later I saw blind eyes open. What I came to understand was that the blame game is really a denial of our identity in Christ. An angel did not manifest to get me out of a fetal position and off the kitchen floor. I was able to get off the floor because I began taking hundreds of truths of who I was in Christ and living from what the Father said was true about me. I picked up my mat and walked. If you can go another week without seeing someone healed through your hands, you will. If you can go another week without growing in the prophetic, you will. If you continue to make excuses of why you do not currently have deep friendship with God, then a year from now you will find yourself in the same exact position with the Father. May you rise up in courage and make the decision to never make another excuse for why you don't have what you have with the Father. His love and kindness has an amazing way of transforming our passion and courage. (See Romans 2:4.) May this be the season where you declare war on any excuse you have for why you are lacking in friendship with God.

CHAPTER NINE

EXPERIENCING BREAKTHROUGH

I have been obsessed with the idea of knowing God most of my life. *Really* knowing Him. I've wanted and still want a true and authentic relationship with Him. At the same time, even the thought of God can be completely overwhelming. I'm sure you've felt that way too. A few years ago a friend of mine told me I needed to listen to a TED talk by Brené Brown. Since I'm really trendy, my response was, "What's a TED talk?" I Googled it and found out that TED stands for technology, entertainment, and design, and TED talks are short presentations—18 minutes long—given at TED conferences. These talks can be on any subject, as long as they have a relevant message for a wide global audience. TED wants to deliver engaging speakers whose presentations discuss new concepts and are supported by evidence. So, with the help of my friend, I stumbled upon Brené Brown's TED talk. I'm sure glad I did. Brené is a professor at the University of Houston Graduate College of Social Work. She has written two different New York Times® bestsellers: *Daring Greatly* and *The Gifts of*

Imperfection. The TED talk that my friend recommended to me has become one of the five most popular TED talks of all time. It is titled, "The Power of Vulnerability." I had no idea that God was setting me up and using a TED talk to do it. Brené's thoughts on vulnerability instigated a radical shift in my heart and mind. As I listened, I knew what she was sharing had dramatic implications in the Kingdom of God. I won't repeat her entire talk for you. I urge you to listen for yourself.[1]

As I listened, a dam broke free inside of me when I realized that down deep in my core it's not possible to have intimacy with God without a high level of vulnerability. Lo-debar thinking always keeps your guard up—it works against vulnerability. At the King's Table, sons and daughters just want to sit next to Papa. We want to be near Him no matter what anybody thinks, and that passion gives us the confidence to be vulnerable. As we grow in vulnerability, His power to impact others for the Kingdom seems to "accidentally" increase in us. I started to see a pattern: vulnerability leads to intimacy with God and others, which leads to a higher level of power in both of those relationships. Where there is no vulnerability, there is no power. It sounds so simple, but the implications are enormous. I started to ask the question: "Is it possible that God is not looking for people to become charismatic—He's simply looking for people to become vulnerable?" As I began to change my thinking and dared to be vulnerable, I also noticed a dramatic increase in the prophetic in my life and ministry.

Vulnerability is the state of being exposed. This realization led me to ask myself a lot of questions about whether I lived my life in a plastic state or if was I truly becoming a person who did not feel the need to guard myself as if everything was always OK with me. As I asked from the perspective of my relationship with God and with other people, I started to notice that some key characters in the Bible showed more vulnerability than I did—and that I could learn from them.

It's one thing to think about God. It's an entirely new thing to begin to believe that you can actually think *like* God. Once we start thinking like God, we begin to see what God sees. When I was younger, I had a hard time reading the Bible. Even though I loved Jesus very much, I could not find the passion to devour His Word. I finally realized in one season of my life that I had grown up with the mentality that the primary purpose of Jesus was to get me into heaven when I died. That mentality— that misconception—worked against me in many ways. I had no revelation that Jesus actually died to reconnect me with the Father. I was completely and utterly shocked to discover that Jesus and His Word were actually an invitation to the King's Table where I can build the deep friendship with Father that He intended from the beginning. When I fully started to believe this, I started to notice principles in the Bible that helped me *metanoia*—transform my mind. The more I allowed God's Word to transform my mind, the more the supernatural realm took on a greater reality than the natural. As that transformation took hold, I began to see more healings manifest when I prayed for people. Breakthrough is a natural outflow of thinking like God. With that in mind, we can see that the story of Zacchaeus has powerful implications.

Zacchaeus' story is the perfect dance of what I call the "Ephesians 2:8 Two-Step," which states, *"For it is by grace you have been saved, through faith—and this is not from yourselves, it is the gift from God"* (NIV). So often we don't see God's power manifest as we minister because we are thinking like orphans. Orphans are not totally convinced that God wants to move on their behalf. When we're living in Lo-debar, we don't yet understand His will, nor do we know what our role is in partnering with Him. We do not know how to dance with grace. When God showed me how to start dancing with Him, I began seeing healings—lots of them. At The Garden Greenville, we are always asking God to show us how to dance with grace. Zacchaeus' story shows us how the dance of grace works. What is so interesting to me about his story is that grace transformed him so quickly that he offered to pay back a lot of money he had embezzled. Jesus did not command him to do that. God's grace impacted Zacchaeus so much that it did not take a command from God for him to respond with grace. Zacchaeus' vulnerability led to a grace invasion that led to transformation. Vulnerability matters in our ability to stay pulled up tight to the Table and in the arena of breakthrough. As a matter of fact, it is the recipe for breakthrough. The reason we do not see more breakthrough in our ministries and in our own lives is that we focus on having huge faith. Jesus said that all we need is mustard seed faith. We don't have faith problems. We have love and vulnerability problems that come from Lo-debar mindsets. That is what's keeping us from breakthrough.

COURAGEOUS VULNERABILITY

Zacchaeus and another Bible character, the woman with the issue of blood, have a lot in common. Both of them knew Jesus was on the scene. Think about this for a moment. Jesus was on the scene for many other people besides Zacchaeus and the woman with the issue of blood, but they received something the others did not. I think they received because they knew how to dance with grace. This woman pulled an Ephesians 2:8 and exercised her faith in Jesus. To her, grace was a person, not a concept. The moment I stopped seeing grace as a subject to be studied and started seeing grace as a person to be embraced, healings began to manifest. Believing in Jesus but remaining in Lo-debar means practically nothing in the supernatural realm. Even demons believe in Jesus. Believing in Jesus is not enough. Pulling yourself up to the Table, having faith in the grace He offers, and knowing how to receive this grace, are incredibly important.

Matthew 9:20-22 shows us that this woman displayed enough vulnerability to receive healing from grace itself. As I've studied healing over the last 15 years, time and time again I've noticed the connection between the faith and the breakthrough. Yet, it wasn't until that short TED talk that God began to show me there is even more in play—that vulnerability is the key. When a person is not guarded, when he or she is willing to lay fears aside and become emotionally exposed, it has an undeniable effect on breakthrough. Perhaps our need for enormous faith is overrated. Maybe it's more important to have courageous vulnerability.

I love when Paul says in Romans 7:15-25 (NIV):

> *I do not understand what I do. For what I want to do I do not do, but what I hate I do. And if I do what I do not want to do, I agree that the law is good. As it is, it is no longer I myself who do it, but it is sin living in me. For I know that good itself does not dwell in me, that is, in my sinful nature. For I have the desire to do what is good, but I cannot carry it out. For I do not do the good I want to do, but the evil I do not want to do—this I keep on doing. Now if I do what I do not want to do, it is no longer I who do it, but it is sin living in me that does it. So I find this law at work: Although I want to do good, evil is right there with me. For in my inner being I delight in God's law; but I see another law at work in me, waging war against the law of my mind and making me a prisoner of the law of sin at work within me. What a wretched man I am! Who will rescue me from this body that is subject to death? Thanks be to God, who delivers me through Jesus Christ our Lord! So then, I myself in mind am a slave to God's law, but in my sinful nature a slave to the law of sin.*

Paul is talking about pride. Perhaps one reason so many of us still live in Lo-debar and don't see more healings is not because of our healing theology, but because of pride. Pride and vulnerability oppose each other. Paul accomplished so much in his life, yet he was incredibly vulnerable. He boasted in something other than himself; he boasted in his weakness. *"If I must boast, I will boast of the things that show my weakness"* (2 Cor. 11:30 NIV). To walk in the power Paul walked in, we must be willing to study and embrace the humility and vulnerability he walked in. There is no way around it. Even Jesus said, *"Don't you believe that I am in the Father, and that the Father is in me? The words I say to you I do not speak on my own authority. Rather, it is the Father, living in me, who is doing his work"* (John 14:10 NIV). Humility and vulnerability go hand in hand. So many people have been turned off by the idea of entertaining anything, like healing, that they miss how being charismatic should not be the goal. Vulnerability should be the goal. I believe that if a new breed of vulnerable Christians rises, we will see all the gifts of the Holy Spirit manifest as we learn to think and posture our hearts and minds differently—as sons and daughters at the King's Table instead spiritual orphans in Lo-debar.

Zacchaeus and the woman with the issue of blood were willing to lower themselves in a posture of humility, creating banks for God's river of grace to flow. Zacchaeus humiliated himself by climbing up a tree to be able to see Jesus. The woman with the issue of blood crawled on her hands and knees to get to grace. The old saying "it's all about grace" isn't exactly right. It's all about learning how to dance with grace. Grace does not transform me until I come to the end of myself, lay aside my orphan mindset, and admit that I need it. Grace is available to all, but only a few experience it. The two men who cried *"Have*

mercy on us, Son of David!" (Matt. 9:27-31 NIV) show us how to dance with grace. They showed vulnerability by following Jesus and admitting their own inadequacies. Grace can be available to a proud man and never affect him. But the moment he says, "God, help me, I can't fix myself," we see healing. Vulnerability is like a suction cup for the miraculous of God. As sons and daughters, we can embrace vulnerability because we can trust that grace will be our landing pad. If we're truly convinced that we are dependent on the Father for everything, then being vulnerable with Him and others follows naturally.

LIVING WITH TRUTH TELLERS

God puts us in relationship with others so we don't boast of anything other than how much we know Him. It is a fact. I want to please my heavenly Father, and sometimes He works through others to help me develop the character needed to fulfill my assignment. We all need a few trusted people in our life who will tell us the truth. I like to refer to the truth tellers in my life as "chocolate-covered razor blades." They get the job done in the sweetest way. I have three. These are people that when I ask them a question or they see me taking on an offense, or acting in a way that is unloving, they call me out. I may not be from a family of runners, but I am in a family of truth tellers. Hear me say this, truth telling is calling out who you are in the Family of God, how He made you—calling out His character in you, His truth. These truth tellers have a critical eye, not a critical spirit. We need people in our life who love us and tell us the truth, based on the Word of God and not their own opinions. They are put in our life to help us develop. King Saul had an assignment, but because of his pride, his ambition, his appetites, and his desire for the approval of man, he failed to see that he was getting off course.

Truth tellers are motivated by love. They are not trying to damage you or break you. They want to help you grow and see you succeed. Truth tellers are patient and know that you are always a work in progress. They are kind and they leave you with hope. They are not envious, trying to break you in order to elevate themselves. They don't boast of how much they "helped" you, or gossip about you or others. They take no pride in their words. Truth tellers love well and are not afraid to help you see through God's eyes and heaven's perspective. They trust God to only reveal what you need to know in the moment. Our big Brother, Jesus modeled this. He spent time with Father, then moved out to love others in power. He left people with hope because He was moved by compassion. He didn't see the woman at the well as a project to fix, like a leaky toilet that had soiled the floor. He saw her as a daughter who had lost her way, believing untruths. When she met Jesus, He told her the truth without destroying her in the process. He reminded her of her identity and set her free. We need wise people around us who know what is required of us, who act justly, love mercy and walk humbly with God everyday (see Mic. 6:8), who help us see our excuses as feeble veils keeping us from the truth. Jesus removed the veil so that we can have direct access to Him. Access to Jesus is access to the truth.

So how do we know the truth? How do we know if what these chocolate-covered razor blades are saying is true? We have two ways to weigh and measure, to judge truth. One is the Word of God, and the other is the life of Jesus. We have been given the great gift of the Holy Spirit. It was through Him that the Word of God was put into written form. Jesus was the Word made flesh, before the earth was even formed. He only did what He saw the Father do, He only spoke what He heard the Father say. He told us to judge the fruit. We can know that the truth tellers in our life are trustworthy by their fruit. Jesus knew the Torah very well; He was a student of the Word, setting an example for us to also be students of the Word. Holy Spirit will always align you to the Word. He is our present day comforter and the power in our life. If the words in your head and heart do not align with the Word and the Spirit, they aren't from God. Set your mind on the truth and you will find a freedom that is too good to be true. The Gospel message of love is for you today. It heals your past and gives hope to your future and the future generations.

FORGIVENESS

I have decided to pull from the legacy of love that is available to me as a believer and leave behind the old. How do we do that? Forgiveness. When Jesus hung on the cross, beaten beyond recognition, He said, *"Forgive them for they do not know what they do"* (Luke 23:34). Forgiveness is not an excuse. It releases us from the sins of another, and the shame of another, and from our own poor choices. Forgiveness is the path to the freedom. It is the way to open yourself to begin to think like your Father, to see from His perspective and not from your wounds. It is a true transformation that goes beyond just moving out of Lo-debar. It is the art of remaining at the Table; the art of building deep friendship with Elohim. It is the ongoing dance; the poem that He continues to write that is the story of your life that brings light into the darkness. It is life lived vulnerably in community without excuses. It is owning your mistakes and saying, "I am sorry," and then working toward not repeating that behavior again. This might sound like striving, but it is really all about not sitting back and waiting for something you have already been given.

The apostle Paul wrote that we are to work out our salvation with fear and trembling. (See Philippians 2:12.) He is talking about Holy Fear, a fear of God who is our Father, whose ways are higher than our own understanding; a fear of God who is the Ancient of Days and knows before He speaks just how He intends the story to unfold. My reverence for Him is my trust in His goodness that is built over time. If you let Him, He will take you again and again into deeper levels of trust, not because of fear, but because as you grow in wisdom and revelation, you are trusted with even greater things. He shares His secrets with His friends. You grow to trust Him and He sees in you a trustworthy son. Trust is built, not given.

A LIGHT HEART

One of the secrets of building deep friendship with God is the ability to have a light heart. If we always associate heaviness with God, we'll miss Him 99 times out of 98. I love humor, laughter, and joy on a consistent basis. I am not talking about some sort of slapstick humor that is juvenile or silly. I'm simply talking about finding the humor in everyday life. Over the years, God has shown me that my ability to operate in the prophetic is directly related to the humor that He has helped me develop. His yoke is easy and His burden is light. There is a direct correlation between having a light heart and having the ability to hear him. Just the other night, I was laughing with some friends and a moment later I got into an Uber and had a prophetic word for our driver. I didn't have to go into some serious religious mode to do it. At God's core there is joy. He carries joy in the midst of seeing all the calamity in the world. If joy never leaves Him, it should never leave us. Please understand I am not associating joy with being irreverent or with weird humor. When I get calls from people in our church dealing with very heavy problems, I don't approach them with laughter. The Bible tells us clearly to mourn with those who mourn and rejoice with those who rejoice. I'm simply suggesting that there is a direct correlation with the ability to live with a light heart and have a deep friendship with God.

HUMILITY

Over the course of my lifetime I have learned so many things about myself, some of which have not been a lot of fun to process with the Holy Spirit. When I was five years old, I had an encounter with God shortly after the death of my grandfather. I was sitting outside on a rock when I heard an audible voice say, "I am going to do great things with your life for my Kingdom." At the tender age of five I had not formally given my life to Jesus Christ for salvation, yet I knew who it was that was talking to me. For whatever reason, I decided not to tell anyone about that experience. I simply kept it to myself. Even now when I think about it, I can remember the scene like it was yesterday.

That encounter was in 1977. The next time I would have an encounter like that was in 1994. I was in Jefferson City, Tennessee, working at a Christian Sports Camp. Late one night while sitting outside by myself in the middle of a ball field, I looked up to heaven and said, "What is it that you want from me God?" I immediately heard His audible voice answer me. He told me what He was going to do with my life. Twice in less than 20 years God gave me a glimpse of my destiny. Both times it was like hearing a message from a friend. It did not even take any faith for me to believe those two different encounters. My hair did not stand up on my neck, I did not see any angels, and neither encounter gave me goosebumps. Truth be told, most of my encounters with God are very simple and matter of fact.

You would think that two encounters like this would leave me few doubts about what it is that God wanted to do with my life. The truth is quite the opposite. It is easier for me to prophetically perceive what God sees in other people than to receive what He sees in me. For example, God gave me a word of knowledge about a friend of mine and his sister that was so accurate that it startled both of us. God told me my friend's sister's name and some other very specific things about her. I heard it so clearly that it did not really feel like I was exercising faith. This has happened so often over the last few years that I've lost count of the number of times God has blessed me and others with so many accurate words of knowledge (see 1 Cor. 12:8). With this kind of ability to hear God for other people, growing in my own identity should be simple. Yet, when it comes to my own perception of how the Father sees me as a leader, I get some kind of spiritual brain freeze. The person that has helped me the most to get over this hurdle is King David.

King David was an amazing man in so many ways. To study his life is to peel back layers. I stumbled upon a very strange verse in First Chronicles 14:2 (KJV) which says, *"And David perceived that the Lord had confirmed him King over Israel, for his kingdom was lifted up on high, because of his people Israel."* This struck me as odd because King David sure did seem to wait a long time before perceiving that he had been established as King over Israel. I mean a long, long time. Did he have a short memory of the many encounters he had already had with God to confirm this? Why did it take so long for David to perceive who God had declared him to be? I mean, Samuel poured oil on David's head, David defeated Goliath, he had success with Judah and yet he still didn't understand who God was calling him to be. Welcome to the journey of most, if not all of the people in the Kingdom of God.

As I pondered the life and times of King David, Holy Spirit led me to a book written by Dale Mast titled, *And David Perceived that He Was King.* Through this book God helped me to identify my strengths and weaknesses regarding operating in the prophetic. I could "see" easily for others, but not for myself. Then came the breakthrough dream about an avocado.

I've had some strange dreams over the years, but the one I am about to describe is at the top of the food chain of strange dreams. Let me set the context before I go into the dream. In 2017 I was privileged to be part of a television show titled *Adventures with God.* The filming involved Shawn Bolz and some other well-known ministers in Orlando, Florida. Darren Wilson and WP Films brought us in to film for a week about the prophetic and some hot topics in the Kingdom. A month before I went to do the filming, I was in my bedroom and I said casually to God, "I sure wish I could hear you like Shawn does." Shawn is the author of *Translating God* and *God Secrets*. He is prolific in the prophetic and uses his gift to train up hundreds of thousands of people all over the world. When I said that to God, I stopped in my tracks because for the first time in my life, I felt a literal sadness come over me from Him. I immediately knew in my spirit something was wrong. I sat down on the side of the bed and said, "Father, I don't know what's going on but I feel like you are literally upset with what I just said to you." Over the next few moments, a stream of consciousness flooded me in my spirit, and this is what He said to me:

> *Chad, you think that it's humility to say what you just said to me, but it's not. You actually are self-dep-recating and not being honest with the gift in which you operate. You see other people through my lens, yet when it comes to seeing yourself, you have confused humility with false humility and self-deprecation. You will limit yourself the rest of your life until you start seeing yourself the way in which I see you. You see yourself as righteous because of the blood of Jesus, but when it comes to who you are in my Kingdom, it's easier for you to look down upon your gift. The enemy has convinced you that this is humility. It saddens me, Chad, to hear you ask me for something as though you*

don't walk in friendship with me and have the ability to hear me every day. Until you remove this root, you will never fully experience what I want from you in the prophetic.

I was startled. It had been quite a while since I had been called out by the Father. Even though His words did not bring condemnation, they did bring a sharp conviction. I had been confusing humility with self-deprecation. I'm not so sure that false humility is not the worst form of pride. That night I went to bed and dreamed that I was laying on my back and a doctor peeled half of my face back with a surgical instrument. With half of my face peeled back, the doctor then pulled a full-grown avocado seed from under my left eye. In the dream I asked, "Am I going to die?" I never saw the doctor's face and he never answered my question. When the avocado seed was removed, I glanced to my left and saw one of my best friends sitting beside me. His name is John Helms and we have been friends for over 20 years. We even went to seminary together. John reached over and helped the doctor put my face back together and suddenly I sat up, looked in the mirror and it looked like the surgery had never even happened.

When I woke up from that dream, God began to immediately download what the dream meant for me. He showed me that He was going to help do surgery on my ability to see and perceive correctly. I was going to start seeing and hearing how He perceives and sees me as a leader. He told me that He had to remove a seed of doubt, and that He was going to use my friend to help me understand that God loves me and wants me to perceive myself the way in which He does. I want what I'm going to say next to be so easy for you to understand that you will have to hire someone to help you misunderstand it. Ready? Until I get a proper perception of who I am in Christ, and who I am as a leader, I will greatly limit what God can do with and through me.

If you read David's story long enough, you can see his progression from knowing very little of his identity, to knowing who he was in God's eyes, to a massive amount of security in his God-given identity. David was even able to help Mephibosheth, one of Jonathan's sons, make the journey for himself. So often we are looking to someone else to impart a gift such as the prophetic to us while failing to realize that this type of growth comes most fully when we are in relationship with the Father. It can begin with a simple prayer such as, "Father, I am asking you to help me perceive how you see me." Simple but profound. What we think is humility can actually be spiritual orphanhood. It gives me great comfort to know that King David struggled with identity issues.

NOTE

1. https://www.ted.com/talks/brene_brown_on _vulnerability.

CHAPTER TEN

ABUNDANT LIVING

Most of us believe that God can train us in the desert seasons, but has it ever occurred to you that He can train you through favor? You may say, "That doesn't fit my theology." Well, perhaps it's time to change your theology to match God's. The world doesn't revolve around the way you think or the way I think. The world revolves around the way He *is.* He was a blesser in the Garden to Adam and Eve. He blessed Abraham, Joseph, David, and Job—yes, even Job. What we need to do is take the stories of His goodness and believe that He loves to bless us, even now.

Jesus said, 19 times, "Let it be done to you as you believe." I'm simply saying, let's get to the King's Table and let it be done to us as we believe, according to His written Word. I am not leaning on someone else's revelation on this. I have dug into the Scriptures for a long time searching out wisdom on abundance. I used to think God made people sick to get glory out of it. Then, 16 years ago, Father asked me if Jesus ever made anyone sick. I searched the Word and could not find anything that said He did, so I had to conclude that He didn't. I read the Scriptures and started believing what the Scripture said, and then? Then, I just happened to see healings manifest. I just happened to start praying in tongues. I just happened to start walking with the Holy Spirit in power. Then God asked me, "Will you let me do with you on abundance, what I did with everything else?" I said "Yes," and He proceeded to take my little Le Sueur pea-brain-thinking self, who loved Him with all my heart, and said, "Chad, if you will let Me, I'll get your Le Sueur-pea-thinking out of your brain and I'll give you My thoughts, because My thoughts are higher than your thoughts." My reply was, "If You'll show me, I'll do it."

I started looking up passages on abundance, prosperity, and provision from the Father, and what I found blew me away. He didn't just give a little bit. He didn't just meet people's needs. From the Scriptures—not from other people's stories—I began to realize that He's a way more generous giver than I ever thought He was. Then, that truth began showing up in my life. God told me to start ordering the most expensive meal on the menu when I went out on date nights with my wife. I tried to cast that demon out. The first time I obeyed, we went to a place with a menu I can't pronounce and I ordered the most expensive meal. Then, I got a surprise the next day. Someone at church came up and said, "The Father told me to bless you with this." The amount they gave me was at least three times the amount I paid for the meal.

How did God break me of my Le Sueur pea-thinking? He had me step into generosity and then generosity started to manifest itself back to me. The orphan spirit may well up and say,

"Be careful with this message, because someone may go and buy some $900,000 car in the name of abundance." Hang on there and realize something—I didn't do anything the Father didn't tell me to do. The Father told me, "When you go on a date with your wife, do this." He did not tell me to go buy a Lamborghini. He didn't tell me to max out our credit cards. I only did what He told me to do. When I obeyed, He blessed us. In the midst of all this, I realized that my generosity matters too. Instead of giving out of obligation, I started giving out of a heart of love. It's undeniable what's happening not just in my finances, but also in my marriage, with my kids, with my friends, in this church, with my family and extended family. I have to ask, has it ever occurred to us that the message of abundance goes way beyond cash? Abundance is not just about money. God's message of abundance affects every area of life. We tend to look at finances because it is an easy indicator of our identity as a son or an orphan. I say all the time at The Garden Greenville, "Show me your checkbook and I will tell you what you value."

This orphan spirit scale is not mystical. What is the orphan spirit? It is a mindset that does not align to the message of royalty as presented in the gospels. I am a co-heir to Jesus. He's called me to be the head not the tail. He has called us to reign with Him. We think it honors God to walk in a high level of character and discipline. He does value this, but what really turns His stomach the wrong way is when we do those things, but our thinking is contrary to His on abundance. He wants to give abundance in all aspects of life; in relationships, generosity, healing, and in intimacy with Him. *All* is available to us. The shift comes when we realize He is the owner. If He says, "Be generous," then be generous. Orphans hold on for fear of never having enough. Sons realize that there is more than enough.

GOD'S WORD—OUR FOUNDATION

I love to create awkward moments and then watch how people respond. There are just some things you can say that guarantee a moment more awkward than a hairless cat. Some things simply trigger people on a deep level and cause them to be stunned into silence. In Christian circles, a conversation on prosperity will do this ten times out of nine.

Prosperity. That word triggers the orphan spirit. What was your immediate response when you read that word just now? Talking about prosperity in the Church brings out some pretty strong emotions in people. I'm not talking about this because I read someone's book. I'm talking about this because of Genesis 26 and the book of John. When you read the book of John, you realize that Jesus is really nice. He never made anyone sick, and He healed a lot of people. He talked about intimacy with the Father, over and over, then He healed people. Our healing ministry at The Garden Greenville didn't start with our own experiences, it started with reading the Word. We just kept reading the gospels over and over, and we started to believe what had been written, and that it was for today. We began by believing His Word—the Word that tells us our Jesus did not die on a cross so we can be miserable and just make it until we get to heaven. The Word promises us that we can do the same things as Jesus and even greater things, because we have the power of Holy Spirit with us. At The Garden Greenville we started to believe that we are loved and that His compassion brings freedom to others who are suffering.

When you build your life on the rock of His written Word, you don't have to be a parasite, always depending on what other people say or teach. You move from listening to the latest feel-good podcast, to actually feeding yourself on the Word and the revelation it brings to you. You don't have to go to someone else to live off of their blood and off what the Father is showing them. I hear people say, "I just don't feel the love of God." Could it be because there's not enough Word operating in them? Read Mark 4:1-20. When the Word gets in you, when the Seed gets in you, when the Seed gets in *us*, the Seed begins to grow. At that point, satan doesn't come to attack *you*, he comes to attack the Seed in you. Jesus basically said that if you do not understand this parable, you don't understand anything. The farmer scatters seed, then the power comes as the seed gets down in the soil.

When there's no power in my life, instead of going from place to place, conference to conference trying to find it, I need to stop and get into the Word so that the Word can get in me. I'm lacking because there is a lack of seed growing in me. It begins with the Seed of the Word. If I am in a love deficit with the Father, turning to someone else to fill that deficit isn't going to do it. There is a better way. Take ten passages about His love and get the Seed down into you. Then, in community, let that seed be watered by other people's words falling on top of the written Word in you. Let the podcasts and conference speakers water what is already growing in you. Over time, you will find that you have fruit. You will begin to believe the Word. You will begin to shape your thoughts according to that Truth. You will have a new confidence, built not on faith, or circumstances, but on the very principles of the Word of God. You can have faith, and you can have faith for a misconception. This is why we need the Word *and* Spirit along with our community of believers to help us stay on the narrow road. You keep getting the Word in you until you reach the point when the Seed begins to take root and becomes so strong that you can't pull it up. I love a prophetic culture, but I don't love it more than a Word culture. It has happened again and again over the course of history—the Holy Spirit lands in a place and a movement is birthed with a strong foundation on the Word, but then it became about the Spirit. We need to understand that it is not either/or—Spirit or Word—it is Spirit *and* Word. The Spirit of God testifies to the Word of God.

I highly value the prophetic and I strive to grow in it every day, because according to First Corinthians 14, as I pursue love, a natural outcome is that I will want to love others, building and encouraging them through the prophetic gift of the Spirit. I value the gifts of the Spirit. But for those of us who call ourselves Christians, our invitation is to honor both the written Word of God and the prophetic word. We need both. Let us walk in a high level of supernatural ministry, doing Father's works, but also with a desire for expository preaching and systematic Bible study. I don't want to check my brain at the door. Jesus Christ had a PhD in the Torah *and* He walked on water. The world is starving for a movement where you actually do not check your brains at the door. Why can you not lay hands on the sick, see them recover, and still have a PhD beside your name? Just because I walk in things of the Spirit doesn't mean I have to scream at you. I don't have to act weird. There's power in the Word. Many times, when people are so crazy loud, it's an overcompensation for what's not inside of them. Get the Seed in you. Treat people with honor. Stop yelling. You can struggle in the prophetic as you navigate the naturally supernatural, but none of us should be struggling in the Word. A culture of freedom, a culture of honor, a prophetic culture where the Holy Spirit is moving—it all builds on the foundation of the Word. If we don't build everything, including the prosperity, abundance, and multiplication message, upon the Word, then we're just a bunch of people getting stirred up about nothing. It becomes about our own opinions, not His.

When the rubber meets the road and all hell invades your life, you're going to have to respond to hell the same way your King did. He responded out of His mouth with the written Word of God. You want to talk about the prophetic? There's never been anyone more prophetic than Jesus Christ, and He did not respond to the devil with a rhema Word. He quoted the logos. The New Testament is primarily written in two languages, Greek and Aramaic. There are two words that are used in the New Testament for the Word. One is *rhema*, which is the inspired or spoken Word. This is when Father speaks to you through visions, dreams, words of knowledge, words of wisdom, prophetic insight, thoughts, and other prophets. We hear this phrase often, "I just feel like the Lord is showing me." That's great. Rhema words are awesome. They help us to see that the God of the universe sees us, and that He is alive and working right now. The other word used in Scripture for the Word, is *logos*, referring to the written Word. Jesus is described as the Word made flesh. We see in Him the intentions of Father regarding how to live out the written Word. The Word of God was first given to the Israelites in the form of scrolls. They so honored the Word that it was kept in the Ark of the Covenant as they wandered through the desert. In another desert Jesus showed us that we now have access to the Word and we can unroll it for ourselves. We do not need a priest to interpret. The Word is ours now. It is ours to use to combat the enemy. A question to ask yourself in any circumstance you face is, "What does the Word say? What was written to me almost 2,000 years ago?" We cannot underestimate the importance of the Word. Heaven is released over you when, with your own mouth you speak the Word of God.

Ask for hunger, then just start reading your Bible. Just begin. If you fail, then get up and start again tomorrow. Keep at it. Write Post-it notes of Scripture and plaster them all over your walls, your bathroom mirror, your desk. Remind yourself of what is true. Be a student of the Word. Seeking first the Kingdom of God includes going to the Lord, your Master, your Sovereign King, in prayer and the counsel of the Word. Prophetic words are good, but the Word of God is our foundation. Seek God and He will answer you. He will show you the way.

HIS LAVISH ABUNDANCE

We have learned that Lo-debar is the land of barrenness, a place of lack, a place of bitterness. It's a difficult place to live. David was King, and he led Israel in 40 years of peace and abundance. When you are connected to the Father, the natural outcome is that His abundance floods you. We know the King's Table is where the spiritual son or daughter says, "I am not an orphan.

I will not make excuses for what I do not have. I will not get offended." In previous chapters, we've talked about indicators that we're growing in sonship. Here's another one: getting out of all-or-nothing thinking. I'm not sure any of us ever fully understand what it is to live as a son. We have a hard time grasping what's offered to us by Calvary. Let's make the concept scalable. If we look to Jesus as our example of a Son, who lived at the 100 percent mark, we can see where we fall. When He was born, Herod tried to kill him. He had no place to lay His head. His number-one disciple could not even stay awake while He was praying in the garden. Jesus had everything you can imagine come against Him and it never deterred Him from His intimate connection with the Father. If that's 100 percent—where coins are showing up in fish's mouths—then 0 percent is Lo-debar thinking—"I never have anything. Nobody likes me. God hates me. He would never bless me." You are back in the land of lack, barrenness, and bitterness. This is one of the reasons we need the Word of God, the Spirit who is the Counselor, *and* community. We need our friends to tell us when we have moved away from truth, when we start to slide back down the scale. If you live isolated from others, always self-protecting, then the enemy can play with you like a cat does with a mouse.

Many believers walk in a high level of character and integrity, but when someone brings up money or prosperity or blessing, walls go up immediately. I believe this is because a lot of us grew up under a distorted paradigm where our theology was formed around the idea that He is "the God of just enough." There's a small problem with this. Yeshua, just a normal-looking rabbi, shows up in the New Testament and changes everything. His coming-out party, in John 2, was the first miracle in the New Testament. At the end of a wedding, when there was no more wine, He told them to go fill up six stone jars with water. Let this sink in for a second here because we are talking about over 700 bottles of wine. They obeyed, then He turned the water into wine. Plus, His wine tasted a million times better than anything the guests had ever tasted. Here's the question: Why would He need to provide that much wine at the end of the party? Why did He make it taste so delicious? Wouldn't that be wasteful? No, it wasn't wasteful. Jesus' coming-out party demonstrates that He is the "God of too much who likes abundance." His miracle did not fulfill a need, it was not a healing, it was not even a prophetic word or the issue of an assignment. His first miracle was filled with joy. It was an indication of abundance. When we go to heaven, some of us are going to be shocked that our houses are not busted up and sitting on nasty red clay. It is so immaculate in heaven, so pristine, it makes Augusta National look like a flea market in Gaffney, South Carolina.

I heard the Father say to me, "Many people will be very uncomfortable when they come up here to heaven." A lot of us would be more comfortable in a one-bedroom flat up there with Him than we would be letting Him lavish His abundance upon us. I truly believe that the highest form of pride is the inability to receive. I think an even higher level of pride is refusing to accept abundance from the One you say you love so much. I don't mean provision. I'm talking about abundance. There's a difference in provision and abundance. Some of us would go over to the huge jars of wine, stick just one pinky in, and say, "Oh God, you're so good." He would say, "Why are you just stinking your pinky in there, son? I made six barrels." Abundance.

It wasn't just those jars of wine. Peter witnessed Jesus provide an unbelievable abundance of fish when previously there were none. (See John 21:1-6.) Simon Peter, a professional fisherman, had fished all night and caught nothing. All of a sudden, the Lord said, "You caught anything?" By the way, if the Father, Jesus, or Holy Spirit ever asks you a question, I guarantee you, they know the answer before they ask you. That's a fact. Simon Peter confirmed he had caught no fish all night. Jesus told him to just throw the net out on the other side of the boat. When I imagine Simon Peter's response to the Lord, it looks like, "Bless your heart. We're professionals and we're telling you, there are no fish." Jesus told him to just throw the net out there. When he obeyed and threw it, the nets filled with fish. It says in the Greek that the nets began to tear. Abundance.

Why is this issue of abundance so important? It's important because it reveals Jesus' nature. When you know the nature of someone, you can predict their behavior. If you don't believe what's revealed about His character in Scripture, then you can be afforded rights your whole life and never experience them because you never align your thoughts to the thoughts of the Father. You never acknowledge just how nice He is, how good He is. I promise you—He is so good. I am constantly overwhelmed by His goodness.

POSTURE YOUR HEART

If God gives me clarity, there's no space in my life for us (God and me) to work out a deep level of trust. When there's a lot of clarity, I get lazy and I won't build trust. Most people become fat and lazy in success. It seems easier, for a lot of people, to steward a lack rather than a lot. The true mark of being a mature follower of God is that He can give you a lot and it will not even faze you. Have you realized that it's possible to be a multibillionaire and be more humble than someone who lives in poverty? It is possible because the posture of the heart is everything.

After God told Isaac to go to the land He would show him, He gave him these promises: "Stay in this land for a while and I'll be with you and will bless you." God's nature is to bless. The conversation on blessing is not about the blessing, it is about the One doing the blessing. Here's what I'm trying to say—if you believe that God truly desires to bless you, don't be shocked when you start walking with Him and He does it. All He is asking for is a little bit of cooperation, to let Him be the way He's wired to be. This truth regarding abundance really triggers the orphan spirit and especially the religious spirit. That's because the enemy wants to convince you that it's more worthy to walk in lack. If you think about it, that just doesn't make sense. Why would you want an okay marriage when your spouse can truly be your best friend? What if the only way you can get to a great marriage is not through Dr. Phil or Dr. Boo-Hoo, or any other trendy route? What if, instead of getting ten people to pray for you, you pray for your spouse? Quite simply, what if you walk so closely with the Father, that He is blessing your marriage?

In whom do you trust? Here is what many of us do; we start screaming at our checkbooks. "I command you to do this, I command you to do that." Maybe the better thing to say is, "I never deserved to get to this King's Table life, ever. I never deserved it, but now that I'm here, I cannot say "thank You" enough. You are the most amazing person I've ever met in my life. Your blessings are chasing me left and right. Surely goodness and mercy shall follow me all the days of my life. I cannot believe how good You are. I cannot believe how good You are. You are so good. We trust You." It's all about Him.

What if God gave you blessings that you weren't even asking for? I can't tell you the last time I've prayed for anything. The Father told us, at our church, that giving would double the year I taught on firstfruits. We did not chase down a marketing person or pour oil on the offering baskets. We simply believed God and taught our people the principles of firstfruits from the Word. Our leadership, the staff and elders, were the first to commit to honor Him in this area. It is amazing to watch what God told you would happen, actually happen. If I am walking with God, I actually believe that if I seek first His Kingdom and His righteousness, all these things will be added. Seek Him first and things get added. That's how it works. For Abraham, for Isaac, and for us.

God had more to say to Isaac: "For to you and your descendants I will give all these lands." God's plan of blessing went way beyond just Abraham and Isaac. God's blessing on your life is not for you only. What if you are in such deep friendship with God that your great-great-great grandson, whom you will never meet until you are in heaven, is still living off the back draft of your blessing? God's nature is to bless. He tells Isaac, "I will give all these lands and will confirm the oath I swore to your father Abraham." I still live off the blessings from Mama Jane. Her faithfulness in building friendship with God has brought a blessing to four generations—her siblings and peers, her son, her grandchildren and great grandchildren. Even when she was in her last days, she continued to bless others. One of her caregivers said she was the sweetest person to the end. How does that happen? It happens when your heart is the soil for His Word to grow and then the fruit you give to others is sweet. You give because you know that it is His nature in you. You can give because you are no longer living in the land of lack.

It's not about setting up a bunch of targets in our lives, things we need to believe for. We just need to believe that God is good and that He is a good giver. Let's chase Him and let all these other things chase us. If you run towards money, it will run from you A lot of times, if you run towards community, community will scatter from you. A lot of people don't walk in community because they are not intimately connected to the Father. I honestly believe in the Western Church we have so created God in our own image we've lost sight of His true character. We don't worship golden calves, we worship our own work, goals, and plans. We chase the prosperity message to get our entitlements. The prosperity message is always being blessed by God to bless others, and it finds its roots in Genesis 12:1-3. It is the message of abundance. You can love because He loved you. You can give because you know He is a giver. You can heal the sick, because you know He wants His people well. He is generous, so we can be too.

When you are intimately connected to the Father, blessing just flows in every area of your life. I can prove this biblically. I've seen people healed and I don't even pray for healing. I just say, "Father, show them Your goodness." His goodness has no bounds. Why would I cast faith to believe something that is the opposite of His goodness? Did you know one of the words used for prosperity in the Old Testament is "dashen" and it can mean, "to make fat." Praise God, He understands me. I really did laugh when I saw that definition. Dashen—to make fat. I love how God is wired. God also told Isaac, "I will make your descendants as numerous as the stars in the sky." Why did He say that? Because that's just the way He is. There is a pattern going on in God's Kingdom, and it goes something like this; "Adam and Eve, I will bless you, go and multiply. Abram, I am going to bless you. Isaac, I am going to bless you. Jesus, go to the earth and redeem the curse of the law. What I started in Abraham, I am going to make better with you. I am going to make a new covenant and all peoples of the earth will be blessed through you, as long as they will just let Me be Me. Let Me be your Father, let Me bless you."

Let's spend some time in Scripture to see this principle of abundance in action. We're going to Genesis 26. Here we find Isaac, one of the patriarchs. He's arguably the least known patriarch. He's got a famous dad, Abraham who is the Father of our faith. Abraham is the one to whom Jehovah said, "I am going to cut covenant with you." Likely the only memory Isaac had of that God story was when the knife was coming at his throat as he lay on top of a stack of wood on a mountaintop. I would like to hear his perspective on that experience one day.

Not only was Isaac's father famous, so was his son, Jacob. Jacob would wrestle with an angel, who most scholars believe was the Lord. After the wrestling match, Jacob walked with a limp, and a nation was birthed. It was a pretty big story, but it doesn't end there. Isaac's grandson, Joseph, is one of the most famous people in all Scripture. As for Isaac himself, he was pretty ordinary. He gets less airtime than any of the other patriarchs—only one very short chapter. If anyone deserved to have orphan thinking, it was this guy. Famous dad, famous son, really famous grandson, and...Isaac, little bitty Isaac in one passage in Genesis. Fortunately, God's blessing doesn't just flow to the famous. God's blessing flows to all His children. The only thing that can stop it from manifesting in our lives is incorrect thinking about His nature.

Isaac faced a time of famine, just as his father did. He went to Abimelech, king of the Philistines and Gerar, and the Lord appeared to Isaac and said, "Do not go down to Egypt." That warning from God should sound very familiar. God's people seem to always be drawn to Egypt. The Father probably has a repeat button in heaven with the warning, "Do not go down to Egypt." Why is that? Because Egypt represents bondage. We would rather accept a form of spiritual slavery that is familiar to us than experience the unknown freedom available from God. We're like an elephant tied to a stick.

God also told Isaac: "Live in the land where I will tell you." He didn't give Isaac much detail on this one. That's probably because the Father is not a big fan of clarity. By the way, does this not remind you of Abraham's story? God tells him, "I know you don't know who I am, but I'm going to bless you and I will bless those who bless you. I am for you. I'm going to cut covenant with you. Everything that I have is yours. You're going to be called my friend. All I need you to do is leave the land where you're currently living and go to the land which I will show you" (see Gen. 12). Now with Isaac, we have "Abraham Part Two." God says to Isaac, "My name is Jehovah. I spared your life many years ago. I thought about you before you were created in your mother's womb. I need you to not live here anymore. I need you to leave everything and go to the land which I will show you." (See Genesis 26.) Not a lot of clarity there either.

LIVING FROM AN ABUNDANCE MINDSET

There is nothing more ridiculous than a good God wanting to bless His kids, and having them say, "No." They say, "Father, this is not what I was taught about You, so take me to that $0.99 menu because I have to be responsible." Perhaps you should take your spouse to an excellent restaurant and apologize for being so responsible. Perhaps what heaven calls faith, we just call being responsible. A lot of times, in the world's eyes, what we call wisdom, God calls unbelief. Recently I was in downtown Greenville and I was shopping for a Camelbak backpack. I found one that I thought was overpriced. When I looked it up on Amazon, it was 30 dollars cheaper online. I walked out thinking, "I need to be wise with my money." A few minutes later I heard this from the Father, "Go back in there and buy that Camelbak. Invest in the economy of Greenville and speak a blessing over the store." It took me a little while to discern that this was God. I wanted to make sure I was not being irresponsible. I went back to that store and did what the Father told me to do, and in the next four days, over 400 dollars was handed to me from two people. I heard the Father say, "Your obedience and abundance mindset triggered this blessing." Perhaps we need to rethink His thoughts on blessing.

Did Jesus really need to make that much wine at the wedding? Did He really need to help Peter catch that many fish? When a little kid handed Him fish and bread, He fed somewhere between 15,000 and 35,000 people...and there was food left over. You can't get to the end of Him. There's no end to His supply. Where He guides you, He will provide for you. So, if He's guiding you to something, step out there. If you step out where He is not guiding, that's not abundance, that's idiocy. He blesses you as you follow, as you go to the land He will show you. It is not the other way around where we say, "Bless me as I make my own plans and go where I want to go, because you are good." Do not be manipulative. Trust is not manipulative. Love is not manipulative.

God promised Isaac that through his offspring, all nations on earth would be blessed. So much blessing—that's His nature. Isaac made the same bad decision his dad had previously made. He thought the men in this new land might kill him to take his wife, Rebekah, because she was so beautiful. So, he told the king and everyone else that she was his sister. Years before, Abraham did this very thing. He thought strangers in a new land would kill him and take his wife—so he told them she was his sister. I guess the apple never falls too far from the tree. Don't limit God by only giving Him subsections of your life. Just simply say, "God bless me, in everything." What if when your kid is struggling with school you respond by blessing the brains of your child to be able to think the way they were created to think? Why? Because that is how God is wired. You can live in the blessing. You can speak blessings too.

The difference between a spiritual son and an orphan is that a spiritual son clings to the Word of the Lord no matter what while an orphan will back off the Word under pressure. That Word of the Lord is both rhema and logos. You can believe Him. If He says go, then go. If He says stay and plant crops, then stay and plant crops. King Saul became yesterday's man when he did not obey the Word of the Lord. Samuel said to Saul, *"You have rejected the word of the Lord, and the Lord has rejected you as king over Israel!"* (1 Sam. 15:26 NIV). This is not a small matter. Elijah did much the same thing. On Mount Carmel he called down fire from heaven. In the very next scene, Jezebel was trying to kill him and he was scared to death. Isaac acted like an orphan, he failed to trust the Word of God and trust the blessing even in circumstances that seemed dangerous. He chose to be his own protector, his own wise counsel.

Sons and daughters stay at the Table. You can reach a point with God where you remain at the Table because of the great revelation of His love and character, not because you have an epic encounter. You simply know God said it, and you stay put until He gives the next direction. Encounters are great. But I prefer revelation. With revelation, I change and I grow. Even Jesus grew in wisdom and revelation. Do you know that you can actually grow to a place in the Father where encounters are not the most climactic point of your journey? His revelation trumps an encounter.

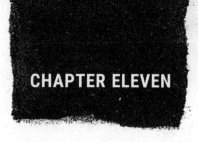

CHAPTER ELEVEN

CHRIST IN US

I have been privileged to lead teams to Haiti six times with Gary Hyppolite and Bethel Mission Outreach who are global partners with The Garden Greenville. These have been wonderful opportunities for me to learn from Gary and help him with whatever he needs to fulfill what God has called him to do. I recall one trip in particular. On this trip, Gary asked if we would like to go on a treasure hunt in the downtown area. I was excited because I absolutely love going on treasure hunts to see what Holy Spirit will do. The thing I love about treasure hunts is that you absolutely have to hear God and act on what He says without "processing" it for weeks and months beforehand. I think that much of the over-planning we do is nothing more than unbelief and the inability to hear the Father's voice and trust Him. The word *processing* has become a hipster word in many circles, and I'm convinced that what we call "processing" God is "unbelief" most of the time. God told Abram to pick up his family and move. He said "yes," and moved. No processing required. I always want to be responsible with what the Father is telling me or the team which I am leading, because if we are not careful, we will take way too long to do what He is asking us to do.

We got on the bus and headed to downtown Croix-des-Bouquets. When we got to the center of town, our team walked over to a basketball court. I immediately heard Holy Spirit tell me to pray for a young man who was a vendor selling water and rice. On his head was an enormous bag that looked incredibly heavy. I told our interpreter Christopher to ask the young man if he had pain in his neck, back and knees. The young man said he did. Right there in the square I prayed for him, and God healed him. This young man told our interpreter that all the pain had left his body. The Holy Spirit told me to pray, I prayed, and the supernatural became more real than the natural in that moment. We hugged this young man, and then Gary said that he wanted us to walk a little bit down the road to the town square where there were more people.

So, after praying for the water and ice vendor, and seeing God heal him, we headed towards Town Square. When we turned the corner and stepped into the Square, I saw "him"—a witch doctor standing on the corner. Our interpreter immediately said, "Don't look at him. Just keep walking." I could tell that some on our team were a little scared. This man had a toy dragon in his hands and different odd ornament necklaces on his neck. The presence of evil emanating from him was very easy to detect. Things were getting "real" in a hurry.

Voodoo is rampant in Haiti. Where I live in Greenville, there's a place called Voodoo BBQ. I would never choose a name like that because I have come to understand just how real and demonic voodoo is. Most Americans don't understand this spiritual reality. As a matter of fact, many Christians think it's silly to even talk about such things. I've heard people say, "You charismatics love the drama of stuff like that." It's not drama. Ask Gary. He knows voodoo is nothing to play around with. Gary would not be allowed to preach in many churches in America because the congregations would either not believe his stories or would simply not want to entertain the idea of such things.

As our team walked around the witch doctor, he began to hiss at us. He did this three times. Christopher our interpreter said, "Let's walk quickly to the square. Don't look at him." At this point, I was in the back of the line, with the entire team of 15 people in front of me. I stopped, turned around and stared at this guy. It made me so angry that the enemy was influencing a man to taunt the team I was leading. As I stared at him, all I could think of was, "the one who is in you [me] is greater than the one who is in the world" (see 1 John 4:4). Christopher asked me, "Do you think the Lord has something for him?" I said, "Yep, let's go." You see, there comes a time when we must simply either believe in the power of life at the Table or not. Not everything is gray. Christianity has to be more than clever whiteboard sessions centered on doctrine and leadership. It has to take action—even in the face of fear. We have to realize that we are working in God's power, not our own; that we are fully dependent on Him.

Christopher and I walked up to the steps where this man was standing. Only one time in my life have I felt a stronger sense of evil. The Lord told me clearly as I was walking up to this man that this was not a situation to play around with. The Lord said, "Chad, he is high-ranking in the demonic." When we walked up to him, he looked right at Christopher, the Haitian interpreter, and said something I could not understand. Christopher looked at me and said, "I'm dizzy. What's going on?" In that moment, I completely snapped with righteous indignation. I looked right at Christopher and said, "I command this dizziness to stop. Father, I ask that You manifest Your presence right now." Instantly, Chris was no longer dizzy. I could tell that something rose up in him too.

I must have said the name of Jesus 40 times over the next 15 minutes. Then I began to pray in the Spirit, which really agitated the witch doctor. I never had any hatred toward the man, but I was furious with the enemy who was influencing him. I couldn't care less how high he ranked in the enemy's camp. In that moment, I did not pray for God to increase my courage or give me revelation of who I am. Sometimes you don't need to pray—you need to simply act. I knew that greater is He who is in me than He who is in the world. I also knew that the same power that is in me raised my King from the grave (see Rom. 8:11). I was locked in at the Table and I realized that the Lion of Judah was alive and well, and all I had to do was release the power that was already in me. When I did this by declaring the Gospel to this man, his demeanor changed. There was no more hissing going on. He would not look me in the eye, and his agitation increased. Paul said that the Gospel is not a matter of talk but of power. The power of God made Christopher's dizziness go away and made the demeanor of this man soften and bow quickly.

I wish I could say that he decided to leave his life of witch-craft and accept Jesus as his savior. He did not do that on that day. I can say that the Gospel was shared with him and it was obvious that he realized he had no power over the unseen Jesus that day. As we talked through this experience as a team, I could tell that quite a few team members realized that the idea of Jesus in us is more real than theory. It's one thing to preach that Jesus is in you. It's quite another thing to believe in that reality and step in the face of a witch doctor steeped in voodoo to prove it. This happened early in the trip, and I noticed that quite a few team members wanted to fight through their own fears and step into who the Father desired them to be throughout the rest of the trip.

Faith is not the absence of fear and doubt. It is stepping right through fear and doubt and moving past what comes against us in our own thoughts. At the time Christopher was getting dizzy in the witch doctor's presence, I had massive thoughts of fear come at me—the kind I have not dealt with in years. At one point, I could feel that dreaded sense of fear in the natural realm. Faith is not waiting till these things are gone. It's simply moving right through our own doubts and fear to step into the place of authority and identity that is ours at the King's Table. It's understanding that our own power will fail, but His power will not. We can only operate in this level of power when we are fully dependent on Him. We all have fears, we all have mis-conceptions, things that we believe that do not align to truth, but we believe them nonetheless. We have blind spots. What we think about ourselves may not align with the truth, both in areas that are strengths and weaknesses for us. We need our Father who art in heaven, we need our big Brother, Jesus, we need our helper, Holy Spirit, and we need family and community.

I believe we make a lot of excuses from ignorance and not out of rebellion. We aren't free because we either don't know the truth or we choose to not believe it. Changing our thinking and moving from being crippled by fear, anxiety and misconceptions requires that we open ourselves up to others and to community. When I say, "open up," I am not saying to become a punching bag for every slander and punch someone wants to throw at you. I am saying that we should be open and vulnerable to others, and when we are, it can lead to even greater understanding of how Father created us and His plan for us. When He searches our hearts, He isn't just searching for the flaws, He is searching for the dreams He has set in us since before we were a glimmer in our earthly dad's eyes.

Some of the excuses we make come from the hurts we experienced from people we should have been able to trust. We make excuses for our own behaviors based on our family trees saying things like, "My daddy was angry, my granddad was angry, and I am angry." We are just angry people at times because of a lack of revelation. I think what could be very helpful is to understand what happened at the cross, and how we are made new when the Spirit of Christ dwells in us. When you accepted Christ and invited Him to reside in you, when you died to your own flesh and then walked on the waters of baptism, when His victory became your own victory, you left the old behind. We need to stop looking at our old family tree as an excuse and start looking to our new family tree and live from there. Your heavenly

Father props His feet on the moon. Your big Brother Jesus conquered death bringing you abundant life and the power to live and to do your Father's works. I know which family tree I want to live from. I am part of God's family and I reside there with a grateful heart.

Many churches blow up numerically because the people are thinking, "If I learn a certain theology, or practice a new methodology and think a certain way, then His blessing has to be mine." That's a religious spirit. God wants relationship, not religion. When you're in relationship with the Father and the blessings are manifesting, you're not running out to touch them, you are not grabbing them, you are not tweeting about how blessed you are. You would rather just stay at the King's Table and thank Him. Because you have learned to be content in all things—when blessings are tangible and when they are not. You have come to understand that it's not all about you. You become a laid down lover. God loves to pick up laid down lovers and give them resurrection power so that no prison cell can contain them. It was inappropriate for the officials to say to Paul, "Now you can be released." He was released when Jesus blinded his eyes on the road to Emmaus. Paul's freedom led him to a life of thankfulness at the King's Table.

If you're not a person of extreme gratitude, you probably don't know what you should be thankful for. Try meditating on the thought that, if not for Jesus Christ, you would rot and spend eternity in hell. I don't know about you, but I'm thankful that is not my future. I'm thankful I get to be reunited with family members. I'm thankful that I have a wife who loves Jesus and goes after Him. I'm thankful that I have three kids who go after the Lord. I'm thankful for my church. I am thankful that I have water to drink. I'm thankful I was raised by parents who love God. I'm thankful for my siblings. I'm thankful that there was money for me to go to my dream school, the University of Georgia. I'm thankful we have carpet. I'm thankful that if it rains, we have a roof that keeps us from getting wet. I'm thankful that we have a place to come worship the Father. I can keep going, but I will just tell you one thing: if this kind of thankfulness is not natural for you, it doesn't make you evil. It probably means that you are still wearing Lazarus' grave clothes. Learn what it means to live to be thankful. Let praise continually be on your lips. When we are thankful, other people want to be around us. Our thankfulness draws others to us and to Him. I read an article three years ago about why people get promoted in the workplace. It's called "the likability factor." It's not competency, or character, it's chemistry. It's the likability factor that gets people promoted. Heaven's agenda is drawn to people who are thankful. You may need to thank someone in your life right now, just for being who they are. Simple gratitude goes a long way. It makes sons out of orphans.

CHAPTER TWELVE

THE POWER OF GRATITUDE

I was pulling into my driveway one day and just started to tear up with thankfulness for everything God had done in my life, everything He had given me—my wife, my children, my house, His Son, and the reality that I get to spend all eternity with Him. Have you ever stopped to really think about that? We are prone to think that He loves other people more than He loves us. That is not true. He doesn't play favorites. You have a lot to be thankful for, if you will just realize it's all about Him and His goodness. This will happen when you sit at the King's Table. When we don't have gratitude, we believe "It's all about me. I deserve more than this. I deserve better." The truth is, we deserve hell. We don't deserve anything more. We don't deserve the breath in our bodies. When we are able to embrace that truth, we will start seeing with the eyes of an owl, a hawk, or an eagle. We will notice things to be thankful for, things other people don't notice. I am not saying we should thank Him in order to manipulate Him. He is brilliant, so that will not work. When you begin to genuinely thank Him out of pure gratitude, you will start to feel the wind of heaven, the downdraft of His blessings. Your gratitude will usher in the favor of God.

Don't allow yourself to become so weighted down by Lazarus' grave clothes that you can't see what to be thankful for. Take the grave clothes off and get out of Lo-debar. Don't search for someone else to pray for you, for someone else to lift the grave clothes off of you or to give you a lift out of Lo-debar. Take them off yourself. Some things are your responsibility, not God's, and not your community's. Develop the perspective of being thankful even in the most difficult of times. Jesus once had thousands of people to feed with only a little bit of bread and fish. The first thing He did was to give thanks to the Father. Then He turned around with enough food to feed thousands of people. Thankfulness positions us for the wind of heaven, the downdraft of His blessings. It's a pattern Jesus demonstrated for life in the Kingdom. We can go through life so unaware. If we could get a glimpse of all the things He has saved us from, we would cry and spend most of our days saying, "Thank You, thank You, thank You."

Imagine if you thanked Him and He replied, "No, thank *you*"? You see, when gratitude is pure, it tugs on the heart of the Father. He'll give you so much blessing you won't know what to do with it. We live in lack when our heart lacks thankfulness. If you struggle with thankfulness, go to His Word, find the places He talks of thankfulness and let them start to sink into your heart. "Know that the Lord is God, it is he who made us. We are his, people the sheep of his pasture. Enter his gates with thanksgiving and his courts with praise. Give thanks to him and praise his name" (see Ps. 100:3-4).

Sometimes we treat thankfulness like it's just a sweet sentiment, but it is so much more. The reason many of us don't walk in freedom is because we don't walk in gratitude. Every gift you have is from the Father of Lights. This is why Paul says he learned to be content in all things. He was content when he was being beaten and when he was not being beaten. He was so connected to God that he could just say, "You know what, if this is the end for me, it's been a good ride. I will be with You forever anyway." If I get to the end of my life and I am petrified and I'm trying to hang onto the earth because I don't want to go, that tells me something. It tells me that I may believe in Him, but I don't really know Him. This is why—when you really know Him, even the end of your life is no big deal. You can say, "Hey, if it ends right here today, I'm going to be with You forever." If you never had another breakthrough in your life, you still have a pretty great ending to the story. Every once in a while, a person just grows up and realizes they don't have to get their identity from their kids or their spouse or their parents or their job. They can be so connected to the Father that if things never changed, they know they've got it pretty good.

The most ridiculous story on the power of gratitude that I can find in the New Testament is in Acts 16:16-40. Paul and Silas were beaten so badly that many scholars believe they probably suffered major swelling all over their bodies. Let's examine what got them into trouble and what they did afterward.

Once when we were going to the place of prayer, we were met by a slave girl who had a spirit by which she predicted the future. She earned a great deal of

*money for her owners by fortune-telling. This girl
followed Paul and the rest of us, shouting, "These
men are servants of the Most High God, who are telling you the way to be saved." She kept this up for many
days. Finally Paul became so troubled that he turned
around and said to the spirit, "In the name of Jesus
Christ I command you to come out of her!" At that
moment the spirit left her* (Acts 16:16-18 NIV).

I love that Paul put up with this annoyance as long as he
could. Then, he turned around and spoke to the spirit. He
didn't speak to the lady, he spoke to the spirit. This is important. Often times what's coming against you is not flesh and
blood, it's a spirit. If you treat the problem as though it's a
person, that problem is going to get worse. Instead, take authority over what's behind that person. Watch what happened when
Paul did this very thing. *"In the name of Jesus Christ, I command
you to come out of her.' At that moment, the spirit left her."* It left
her *at that moment.* Funny how that works.

The crowd then joined in the attack against Paul and Silas.

*When the owners of the slave girl realized that their
hope of making money was gone, they seized Paul
and Silas and dragged them into the marketplace
to face the authorities. They brought them before
the magistrates and said, 'These men are Jews, and
are throwing our city into an uproar by advocat-
ing customs unlawful for us Romans to accept or
practice.'*

All things seemed to be against them at that point. The magistrate ordered them to be stripped and beaten with rods. It was pretty intense. *"After they had been severely flogged, they were thrown into prison and the jailer was commanded to guard them carefully."* What would you do if this happened to you? A spiritual orphan would bicker and complain. A spiritual son would remain in a posture of gratitude.

After they were beaten, Paul and Silas were put in an inner cell, the deepest part of the prison. Upon receiving such orders, he put them in the inner cell and fastened their feet in the stocks (see Acts 16:24). If ever an orphan spirit could have manifested, that was the time. So, what did Paul do? *"About midnight Paul and Silas were praying and singing hymns to God, and the other prisoners were listening to them. Suddenly there was such a violent earthquake that the foundations of the prison were shaken. At once all the prison doors flew open, and everybody's chains came loose"* (Acts 16:25-26 NIV). Their praise became a weapon that set them free! When you are so deep at the King's Table, suffering and persecution don't seem the same to you as they do to a spiritual orphan because you know you don't deserve anything in the first place.

Louis Armstrong was right—it is a wonderful world, but you've got to see it for what it is. Paul and Silas did. They were tied up, yet saying, "What a wonderful God, what a wonderful world!" Then, all of a sudden—BAM! Chains were loosed and they could go free. But did they? If that had happened to a bunch of charismatics, many of them would run around yelling, "I'm out of my prison! I got what I asked for! I'm out of my prison! I got what I asked for! There's my breakthrough! I sowed my seed and got my breakthrough." But that's not what Paul and Silas did. They just kept singing.

> *The jailer woke up, and when he saw the prison doors open, he drew his sword to kill himself because he thought the prisoners had escaped. Paul shouted, "Don't harm yourself, we're all here." The jailer called for lights, rushed in, and fell trembling before Paul and Silas.*

Gratitude is powerful. People tremble at a person of deep gratitude. Pray for the courage to be a person of gratitude.

When you have deep friendship with God, the enemy trembles. The praise of Paul and Silas drew others to the God they were worshipping, causing the jailer to ask them, *"What must I do to be saved?"* (Acts 16:30). Their reply—

> *"Believe the Lord Jesus, you will be saved, you and your household." Then they spoke the word of the Lord to him and all the others in his house. At that hour of the night the jailer took them and washed their wounds; then immediately he and all his household were baptized. The jailer brought them into his house and set a meal before them; he was filled with joy because he had come to believe in God—he and his whole household. When it was daylight the magistrate sent their officers to the jailer with the order: "Release those men"* (Acts 16:31-35 NIV).

I can imagine Paul saying, "I've already been released. You don't need to release me. I wasn't really bound up in the first place."

Jesus could have called down legions of angels when He was on that cross. He was tied up and accused of a crime He didn't commit, but even then, He kept his mouth shut. Why? Because His identity was determined at the King's Table, not by what was around Him. Jesus had the authority to walk right out of there, but He didn't. Instead, He embraced the cross because that was His assignment. When you are at the King's Table, prison seasons will come and go and some may even come directly from the hand of the Father to groom you more in the image of Jesus Christ. You trust Him in and out of the prison seasons.

I'm afraid much of the Church has little understanding of this message of suffering. When the Father sends you into a tough season, both of you will see what you are made of. Paul is called the greatest overcomer of all time, other than Jesus Christ by most biblical historians. Some of you reading this book have tremendous destinies in your future. In order to get there you have to overcome whatever is standing in your way. It's easy to thank Him when things are flowing. However, if you can't thank Him from the prison cell, when the doubts are invading and things aren't going your way, then the concept of gratitude might not yet be fully real to you. Learn to thank Him from prison, when your faith waivers, when you cannot feel His presence, in the midst of your pain. Thank Him just because you're so thankful you can't help yourself.

One night when I was preaching in Tennessee, I told God, "You are incredible." He replied, "I think you are incredible too." When we act like Him, it thrills Him and even brings rewards that perhaps we have not considered. The things that look like heaven manifest in our lives because of gratitude. These things show up in our marriage, with our kids, with our finances, and with our protection. They're all ushered in by saying, "I want to say thank You." We have so greatly underestimated the power of gratitude. I believe gratitude is the number-one weapon in the Kingdom. Psalm 100:4 says that we are to enter His courts with thanksgiving. Have you ever given serious thought to the benefits of genuine thanksgiving? A few years ago God began to show me the power of gratitude. I have seen God move in my life from victory to victory without me even praying for breakthrough. This has happened over and over again. As a matter of fact, He began to give me revelation on how He fights battles on our behalf that we are not even aware of when we are walking in true gratitude. One night I was struggling with a decision that I needed to make in leadership and I said, "Father, I cannot discern what it is that you want me to do." He said, "Worship me and you will know what to do." The Father loves gratitude. He loves thanksgiving. He is not drawn to a critical spirit. Gratitude is a hallmark of spiritual maturity. The highest form of spiritual warfare is genuine thankfulness before God, because He will defeat your enemies for you if you just remain thankful. He will defeat enemies you don't even know you have. Why would you enter His courts with bickering and complaining? Why would you spend time reminding God of what He hasn't done for you? A high form of wisdom asks, "Do I walk out gratitude, or am I more known for bickering about the manna?"

A strong indicator of a true son or daughter sitting at the King's Table is they just can't stop thanking Him. They're always telling Him: "You are so good. You're so good. You're just so good." This is thanksgiving coming from a pure heart, with no desire to manipulate God. It comes from a pure place of gratitude and can open doors you never even thought to intercede for. What if you just start being thankful and then ten years from now, you turn around and say, "How did so much favor flow in my life?" What if it's because of two things: God is good, and you tugged on that grace with your faith and genuine thanksgiving? For example, a lot of people get tripped up on finances, because they do not bring their firstfruits to the Father and present them at their local church. When you bring your firstfruits and offer them to Father, it is more than just words. Your firstfruits are an offering of thanksgiving. Spiritual orphans say, "God, I've been disappointed in you for so long in my life. It is all about me and You never come through for me. I'm in Christ, thank goodness for heaven. I guess I'll see you there whenever." Spiritual sons and daughters say, "Father, you're too good, you're just good. Thank you so much. If you never did another thing for me, I've got it pretty good. When I leave my body, I'm going to be with you forever. This is too good to be true. You are awesome. You are awesome, God."

We don't wrestle against flesh and blood. If you're bumping into someone who is grumbling and engaging in divisive issues or behaviors, they may not even know that they're being used by the enemy to stir up conflict. I'm not talking about people outside of Christ. You can pray in tongues and walk in no character and be used by the enemy worse than someone who does not know the Lord. In my dream, God was saying, "Don't ever harp too much on strategy. Don't try to figure this thing out.

Just be like Jehoshaphat. Put the worshipers in front. Put the people full of gratitude in front and I'll do the rest."

When we thank Him from the Table, it's not just for Him to say "Oh, you're welcome." Thankfulness actually releases the angelic realm into our lives; it releases breakthrough. Thankfulness actually wars against the enemy. Let me say it this way—when one of my kids tells me, "Hey dad, I just wanted to say thank you," it actually makes me want to multiply what I've already given them and give them more.

Why is the Bible always reminding us to give thanks to Him? Because thanks produces genuine humility. Saying "thank You" every day reminds us that we didn't bring ourselves into this world. We came from Him. Everything is about Him. He deserves all my praise. I come to Him just because I'm thankful, not because I'm looking for Him to give me more things. Humility is not self-deprecation; it is recognition of His greatness. It is recognition of Him. Am I going to chase God for a platform? No. I am going to chase after a close seat at the King's Table because He's just good. I want to be as close to Him as possible. I want to be like the disciple John. I want to lean into His chest. I want to be so close it makes angels nervous. Honestly, we should be so close to Him that we are triggering the religious spirit every single day. I don't want to just be in the vine. I want to be deep in the vine. My body is decaying every single day, but there's never been anything decayed about Him. He's always existed. No one made Him. He told the sun, "You will be that big. You will be this hot, and I'm going to cause you to rise every single morning. I will make the moon my footstool—I am going to prop my feet up on it." He is Lord God Almighty, Jehovah. Every once in a while, we ought to say, "You are big. Thank You for being You." If you don't think you have anything else for which to thank Him, then at least thank Him for Jesus. Jesus was His firstfruits given to you.

CHAPTER THIRTEEN

HUNGER

I have noticed one common trait in every single place where God has poured Himself out over the years—people simply hunger for His presence in a way that could be considered extreme. I believe hunger is a gift and that it is also contagious. I also believe that many churches don't follow the ethos of Jesus. They choose to eliminate the works completely, cherry-picking which parts of the Word they want to follow. Jesus Christ focused on three things during His ministry on the earth—He taught the Kingdom, healed the sick, and delivered people of demons. In America, it's possible to have a successful ministry and not focus on any of those three things. Is this sincerely ok? I don't believe it is. We should desire His presence more than we desire our next breath. Many in Church today do not know that there is a supernatural place they can tap into now. Others know, but they choose to walk away because when God's Spirit comes, things can get messy. At The Garden Greenville, I see a body of people yearn for the garment of Jesus Christ in the way the lady with the issue of blood did. I see people with a pure and simple desire to see Jesus pour Himself out the way

He did when He walked the earth. Jesus hasn't changed—we have. Honestly, it's undeniable that hunger, especially corporate hunger, moves people to get into a position to receive extraordinary things from God. Hunger matters. People who want to walk in the works of the Father (John 10:38) need a level of aggressiveness. Until you want a culture at your church that is naturally supernatural more than you want your next breath, you'll probably never see it manifest.

Jesus lived a life of discipline. His ethos was to rise early. Many scholars believe that He spent three to four hours in prayer daily. He memorized the Torah. Was it boring? Or was it hunger? Both can bring breakthrough. If Jesus, fully God, deity, came to the earth and still needed hours daily with Papa, then why do we think we don't need the Word and times of seclusion. Building friendship with God includes making time and space for Him. What many people call extreme, God calls normal. Jesus was prepared by God for 30 years before He was released into public ministry. He worked a job. He was in a family. He studied. He prayed. He developed an ethos, a rhythm of discipline and of rest and solitude. During this time He grew in wisdom and revelation. At 30 years of age He had more intellectual knowledge than He did at 12 when He was found in His Father's house.

Is it extreme for someone living in today's world to read over 100 books a year about people who have been used greatly by God in the Kingdom? It all depends on what we call extreme. I believe leaders are hungry readers who want to learn from others. My love for reading biographies and historical accounts of the moves of God, even the ones that went wonky, has continued to increase my hunger for more of God. It is extraordinary to watch Father land on a group of people who have chosen to be led by hunger, not convenience. Every move of God starts with a group of hungry people. In Wales, before the Revival broke out in 1904, a group of young people were diligently reading the Word and spending time in prayer and worship, night and day. The sounds of worship that came from that period can still be heard in our modern worship songs. God goes to unlikely places like Nazareth, Los Angeles, Wales, Toronto, Redding, San Francisco, Brownsville, and even Greenville S.C. He pours out His Spirit on the hungry, those who die to selfishness. Hunger and humility are a magnet for the Holy Spirit.

I'll never forget one day during my seminary days when I walked into Beeson Divinity School's bookstore and picked up a book on the history of world revivals. I remember that it was January, and the weather outside was awful. I even remember what I was wearing—which never happens to me. That day, I told a friend that I was going to hang out in the bookstore for a while, and then catch back up with him later. Later ended up being about six hours.

I picked up a book and read the story of William Seymour, and before long I was crying. William Seymour was an African American pastor with Louisiana roots whom God moved to Los Angeles, California. William never saw revival coming. A humble nobody from nowhere, he was the son of a slave who became the point guard of the biggest outpouring move of God that the United States has ever seen. He was used by God to lead what became known as the Azusa Street Revival. All heaven broke loose on April 9, 1906, in William's small church in Los Angeles—including signs, wonders, healings, miracles, and people being baptized in the Spirit and filled with power. Azusa looked a lot like Pentecost in the book of Acts. The power of God was on full display. That January day, as I sat on the floor of the bookstore weeping, I said to God, "I want to be a part of seeing you move in unprecedented ways. Please, use me however you want to."

Revival was a theme of my seminary experience. During my first semester, I encountered a man who had a savage passion for revival. Dr. Lewis Drummond was in his 70s when I met him. His beloved students called him Lewie. People often joked that Dr. Drummond could lead an oak tree to Jesus Christ. The man never met a stranger, and he passionately talked about Jesus as though his very life depended upon it. Dr. Drummond taught a one-hour elective course on the Keswick Movement, and I decided to take it. To say that it stirred me up is an understatement. I was like a yellow jacket in an empty coke can. In this class, we studied some of the great moves of God over the years. When we talked about the move of God at Azusa, I became overwhelmed. I remember my right hand was shaking and I felt literal electricity flowing through my body. I was ready to run through a brick wall or two. Dr. Drummond looked at me one day and said, "Son, give Him all you have. Give Him all you have."

All these years later, I find myself even hungrier for revival than I was as a young man. I've seen a lot of people whose passion for Jesus and His Kingdom wanes over the years. The opposite is happening to me. I never want my desire for God to decrease one ounce. As a pastor, I have no desire to play church. I am not interested in slick programs, church marketing, church growth strategies, catchy slogans, or any form of religiosity. I am going after awakening and asking Father for the wisdom and revelation on how to play any role that He has for me to help steward what He wants. I know I want to develop a culture of family, of community, a culture that honors the Word and the power of Holy Spirit. I am all in. I want to develop disciples like Jesus did. I have learned that all of these things require much of each one of us. I want my life to look like Jesus, not eliminating anything. I want intimacy, connection with the Father—to wisely seek Him in all I do, obeying quickly, hearing Him, speaking His words, seeing His works on the earth, and making disciples as I go. The more that I lean into these things, the more God is showing me the power of consecration. In the end, no human has ever been able to control what God does or even how He does something. While this reality is true, my continued walk with God reveals that none of us have complete control over two things: our consecration and our level of that consecration. Consecration means letting go, being willing to be free of anything that does not look like Jesus.

TEACH THE KINGDOM, HEAL AND DELIVER

Being a disciple of Jesus Christ means seeing power in operation regularly, like we see with Jesus' disciples. I believe that what many people call discipleship in the Western Church is actually consulting. There is nothing wrong with consulting, it's just not discipleship. Paul said that the Kingdom of God is not a matter of talk but of power (1 Cor. 4:20). Discipleship means being as interested in the Father's works as Jesus was. Healings and deliverances were not a subsidiary part of the ministry of Christ, and should not be for us, either. At some point, we need to face our own inadequacies with this aspect of discipleship with vulnerability and courage instead of running from the conversation and building theologies and methodologies around things and ideas that oppose who Jesus is and what He taught.

I love the idea of unity, and I pray for it regularly, but I do not ignore the trend in the history of the Kingdom of God that when Holy Spirit shows up in power, division rather than unity is more often the result. Perhaps Jesus was onto something when He said, *"I did not come to bring peace, but a sword"* (Matt. 10:34). When I look back at the history of the Church, I can't help but notice that Holy Spirit does not mind leading people who are in love with Him straight into conflict. I have often pondered this in order to understand it, and I have come to believe that to God, conflict is not a bad thing at all. Conflict actually reveals what is inside us. I believe the enemy leaves many churches alone because they are not much of a threat to his kingdom. I can promise you that if, under the grace of God, you get a culture up and running that sees the Father's works manifest, you are sure to bump into the enemy often. If you want to build a naturally supernatural culture at your church or in your community, you should start with a sober and honest reflection of whether you truly desire this. Counting the cost is wise and necessary.

When I decided that I would rather walk with God—doing the things that His Son did while He was here—than call myself a pastor and not do two of the three things Jesus did while He was in ministry—I had a strong hunch of what it would cost me. Even so, I said yes. I believe a strong, measurable indicator of our relationships with God is obedience. When God cracked the door to the prophetic for me, I peeked in and said, "Yes, I want this no matter what." Now my passion is to help churches and pastors who are skeptical learn how to open that door. I want to help turn their influence into something that resembles what Jesus did while He was here. Most of the battle is about deciding up front that the cost is worth it. If we will take a baby step toward the things that God is passionate about, then He will scoop us up and help us more than we could ever imagine as we go about building naturally supernatural cultures. He cracks the door and invites us to step in. Once we step in, the ball starts rolling. Once the ball starts rolling, the enemy begins to have an "uh oh" moment. I believe that it is time for the enemy to have a lot of "uh oh" moments. I desire to give my life to see normal churches full of normal people begin to believe and understand that God will use any of us to build these naturally supernatural cultures wherever we are. He wants us to know that it can be fun, exciting, and a great learning experience. There is nothing like praying for someone who has some incurable situation and watching God help that person.

OBEDIENCE

I am convinced that what we call processing, God calls disobedience. There are times in your assignment when He gives you a window of opportunity to respond and then moves on to the next person. You can literally lose your assignment by not being willing to say yes, then do your work as to the Lord. He will test you to see just how far He can stretch you. He may even give you assignments that seem ridiculous. Just as I as a father like to reward my children when they do something and do it well, so our heavenly Father likes to encourage and bless our obedience. I have done some crazy things in obedience to God, even things I said I would never do, like pastor a church. God spoke to me one day and said, "Son, I want you to fly to Azusa Street, lick the ground, and fly back to The Garden Greenville and spit on the ground three times." For a guy who grew up in a Baptist church, I sure have come a long way, I guess. So, I got on a plane and flew to Los Angeles to the famous site of the great outpouring of God that started on April 9, 1906, when heaven broke loose in the City of Angels—Los Angeles, California. As I sat on a bench and looked around, I reflected on why God had me fly out to Los Angeles to be at Azusa. The place where the church was located is now an office complex area with only a few plaques that remind people of what happened in downtown Los Angeles. I did not have any goose bumps or deep spiritual revelations as I sat there. I was mostly so incredibly grateful for Pastor Seymour and the people who led that move of God for so many years. I thanked God for their lives and impact, and then I prayed two things. First, I asked the Father to literally guide me to where the front of the church was 110 years ago. Second, I asked Him to use The Garden Greenville in Greenville, South Carolina, to help a lot of people find what people found at Azusa more than 100 years ago.

Ten minutes after I prayed, I sensed the Holy Spirit wanted me to walk toward a specific part of the office complex. As I walked, I stopped and knew that I was standing in a very important place. With a security guard looking on, I got down on my knees, licked the ground of one of the most important places in American church history, and said, "God, I'm all yours. Use me however You want. I really want to know You as a friend." Then, I flew back to Greenville. Soon after I arrived home, I got down on my knees in the middle of the property of The Garden Greenville and spit three times. No angels, no thunder from the sky, and no deep revelations happened. I simply knew that I was being obedient to what the Father wanted me to do. I've learned a few simple things in my years on this earth. One of them is that I can't control what God will do, but I can always control my level of obedience to what He is calling me and my family to do. I don't know why I was supposed to lick Azusa Street and spit on The Garden Greenville's campus, but I obeyed. Maybe someday I will have more revelation.

We here on this team and in this family simply want one thing: we want to see God move powerfully. This is not a trite little saying to us. We sincerely desire awakening, and we are asking God to start with us. I think back to the day when I cried when reading the story of Azusa. The passion I had that day is the passion I have now. I want to see God move in unprecedented ways in my life and sphere of influence. I have no desire to play church. I want to see God do the things through us that He did through Jesus. John 14:12 has to be true. We as a team have counted the cost and are comfortable with whatever comes our way. He's worth it even though pursuing this is a guarantee that the waters will get choppy.

WORD AND SPIRIT

At the time that the Kingdom of God was breaking out at Crossroads Community Church in Greenville, I was serving as an itinerant minister and a co-founder of Wayfarer Ministries. I preached at youth camps and conferences, wrote curriculum for churches, and served on the preaching team at Crossroads while all this Holy Spirit activity manifested. I was simply excited about seeing the things that Jesus saw. In the early days, I got so excited when I saw someone healed that I could barely stand it. I grew up with the view that God was a mean and distant person, and now I was watching Him heal people, sometimes quite dramatically. I'm still not over it all these years later. He is amazing, and I can't wait to see Him one day. He is the nicest person I've ever met in my life. As a matter of fact, when you begin to realize how nice He is and start seeing people healed left and right, you will not care much about the people who come against you. When you have the revelation in your heart that the God of the universe has a picture of you in His wallet, nothing else ruffles your feathers like it used to.

After a few years, God called me to join the staff of Crossroads Community Church as a discipleship pastor. I went through another major crisis, this time not of identity, or sonship, or the supernatural. This time I was slammed in the face with the recognition that we in the Western Church do a lot of work *for* God, but we don't do a lot of work *with* God. We have programs that benefit people, but we do not disciple them in the naturally supernatural ways of Jesus. We tend not to introduce them to Father and to their place at the Table. My crisis involved not just me building my own deep friendship with Father, or me learning to step out in faith and heal the sick, or me growing in the gift of prophecy. The questions that I began asking myself were, "Am I making disciples? Am I bringing others to the Table? And am I helping them to develop into disciples in all the ways of Jesus. If I love God, am I loving others enough to invite them in?"

Crossroads Community Church went through many major changes. There was a change in leadership, and a name change to City Church. Thus began a transition from being a Word church to becoming a Word and Spirit church. As I was busy on my personal journey of discovering what true discipleship means, the lead pastor resigned. Growing up, I had told God that I loved Him very much but I did not want to be a pastor. I have always enjoyed traveling and speaking and meeting new people. That was my comfort zone. The thought of being in one place pastoring seemed like a nightmare to me. Most pastors I knew stayed exhausted and were not the happiest people in the world. Well, God has His plans. When the elders offered me the job, I said, "OK, let's give it a go." I had zero experience in pastoring a church. I had been preaching for 20 years, but we all know that is only a small part of pastoring. In my first meeting with the elders I said, "I probably should not say this at my first meeting, but God told me that we will be moving soon." There was an awkward pause, and then we laughed a little. One of the elders asked, "Where are we moving?" I said, "I have no clue." We were to learn that the Promised Land becomes visible as we walk.

Shortly after that, God gave our former pastor, Steve Keyes, a dream that I was pastoring a church in our town called Mt. Zion Fellowship. I looked right at Steve and said, "Who is in charge at Mt. Zion?" I knew in that moment that God was merging two churches: City Church and Mt. Zion Christian Fellowship. Mt. Zion's pastor had recently resigned. They had 40 acres of land and a building, but no pastor. The church's core had dwindled to around 50-75 people. In a room that seats 500, this crowd seemed quite small. With another pastor from our church, I drove over to meet with Jack and Amonda Hancock. This couple in their 70s had helped found Mt. Zion Fellowship over 30 years earlier. Mt. Zion started as a Bible study in their home in the 1970s. The Hancocks have a history of Spirit-filled living. Amonda's dad was actually a traveling healing evangelist back during the heyday of the healing movement in the 1950s. When we met with the Hancocks, we knew that God was up to something. We both sensed very quickly that God was calling us to merge churches. We had people and needed to expand, and Mt. Zion had a building that needed people. We both had the common vision of wanting to help people build deep friendship with God and one another.

I can't tell you how many people warned me against merging churches. I heard every horror story you can imagine about the dangers of merging. Yet, as I heard reservations from others, God kept telling me that the merger would be like a hot knife through warm butter. His grace was all over this merge. When

God gives you an assignment, He makes a way. I cast vision for both elder boards and said, "We will be called The Garden Greenville. We will be a church that stands in the radical middle of the Word and Spirit. We will be a church that is passionate about being naturally supernatural." I told the elders of my long-term plan to build a healthy environment of discipleship where we train people how to live in the ways of the Kingdom while operating under a strong revelation of the Word itself.

I've noticed over the years that there seems to have been a divorce in the Church between the Spirit and the Word. I wanted to pastor a church that honored both. In the years since the merge, we realize that we are watching that dream turn into a reality. The Garden Greenville is becoming solidified as a church that takes His Word seriously and that is also passionate about operating with Holy Spirit and being open to all of His works. If we go too long around here without a story of miraculous breakthrough, we get antsy. We want to honor the places and people of the past who saw God do impossible things, but we are tired of just reading old stories. We want God to show off here. We want to see incurable diseases healed and people set free constantly. It's not because we read some person's book on charismatic theology. We desire this because we find Jesus, in the gospels, passionate about these same things. Healing is not our idea—it has always been God's idea.

CHAPTER FOURTEEN

LIFE AT THE TABLE

I traveled for 15 years to serve God and make a living for our family. When you travel somewhere and speak to 50 or even five thousand people, you are a hero. They don't get offended with you because you're only with them for a few days. You are a rock star, like Bono. It's not the same when you come back home. It's really not the same when you pastor a church. That rock star effect isn't there when you are preaching and teaching and doing life with people who are very familiar with you.

When I took the job as the Lead Pastor of The Garden Greenville, no one, not even God, gave me a heads-up. I could have used one because He taught me, in the first three years of pastoring, that many Christians in the Church walk in a high level of offense on a constant daily basis. This is a very uncomfortable truth that we have to deal with in the Church. I'm not just talking about your spouse or all the lost souls out there. I'm talking to all of us. If you wonder where you are on the sliding scale between Lo-debar and the King's Table, there is one ginormous question that can lead you to your answer. How easily are you offended? I'm talking about being offended in every area of your life—home, work, church, family, travel, community—all of it. How strong is the spirit of offense in your life?

Now, think about this next question. How easily offended was Jesus? They beat Him beyond recognition. Most scholars believe you could barely tell He was human because He was beaten so badly. That would seem like a pretty good cause for offense. Yet, with His last breath, with teeth probably broken or missing, and with a bloody mouth, He prayed, "Forgive them, they don't know what they're doing. Abba, forgive them." (See Luke 23:34.) That is how Jesus Christ handled offense. As a Christian—a Christ-follower—that is the lead we should follow. Being a Christian is more than just going to heaven when we die. Jesus came to earth to reconnect us to Eden, to reconnect us to His Father, to provide us a seat at the King's Table. He is the bridge to Father. If I'm with Him at the King's Table, am I really going to be walking around every day offended? If your answer is anywhere in the realm of "yes," then you are likely headed back toward Lo-debar, if not still living there.

IT TAKES COMMUNITY

The things that I am sharing with you are not just theories. I have lived through this. The story of offense is my story. The friends I did life with 20 years ago would probably not believe it if they heard me talking about getting over it, about not living in offense. Back then, you could look at me wrong and I got offended. If you said something negative, it would take me two weeks to get over it. What I am sharing with you is very real to me. Go with me to the desert for a moment if you will. In Matthew 4, we find Jesus hungry and weak, and the enemy is there to tempt Him. Satan came at Jesus in three ways: he came after His ambition, His appetite, and His need for approval. I always thought that my big struggle was appetite. Going to Moe's for me is a big deal. Seriously, I get excited about cheese dip. If I looked at the three temptations Jesus faced—ambition, appetite, approval—I would have said, "well, my weakness is appetite, no doubt." Struggling with ambition did not register with me, even when I was processing this with the Father. I could have put my hand on a lie detector test and declared that, "The approval thing in me is dead." I had a serious blind spot, which is why we need community. You are not as good-looking as you think you are, and you are not as smart as you think you are. I don't care how close to the Father you think you are, sometimes you need the Holy Ghost, Jesus, the Father, His angelic revelation, *and* your friends to call a timeout in your life. This is true for everyone, especially me.

I wouldn't be surprised if Father has said to the Holy Spirit, "Let Me talk to Chad," and then Father went back to the Holy Spirit and said, "Let's get Jesus involved with this one, and even a little angelic ministry. And you know what else? I am going to breath on four or five of his friends and they are going to talk to him too, about this approval thing." The whole time this conversation was going on, I was just there talking about sonship, and the healing that comes from recognizing your identity as a son, and how much Father loves you. I was totally unaware of my own glaring blind spot. When it comes to breakthrough, there is nothing more embarrassing and nothing more amazing than for God to show you something about yourself that you literally don't see. It seems to me that amazing should beat embarrassing every time. I believe that embarrassment is why people avoid community. They may say, "God is just calling me to be alone in this season." No, He is not. God is not alone; He is plural. God is community. He said, "Let *us* make man in *our* image." The Lord may want you by yourself for a couple of days, but let's not make that 32 years. Sooner or later, you have to ask the question, "Where am I?" and be willing to hear the answer. "Where am I? Am I worshiping the Father in a corporate setting but wearing grave clothes the whole time? Am I singing for something I want, but there is no evidence of it in my life?" Sometimes the things you preach the hardest and you talk about the most are the very things you're reaching for because you don't currently have them. For example, I preached this passage about 18 months prior to my blind spot being revealed and I had no idea it was about me.

THE THIN PLACE

Just as Jesus was coming up out of the water, he saw heaven being torn open and the Spirit descending on him like a dove (Mark 1:10).

What if tomorrow morning, you're going about your normal day, and heaven opens up, you hear an audible voice, and the Spirit descends upon you? That is a dramatic God encounter. I had a tremendously abnormal encounter with God in 2014. I didn't come up out of water to see heaven opening. As a matter of fact, I was just in my den. It was 2:30 in the morning, my wife was asleep on the couch and I was typing. We even had a fire going because it was winter. It was a great Nicholas

Sparks-type moment. I'm not being casual about this because I do not hear the audible voice of God all the time. Angels don't manifest in my room on a rhythmic pattern. If you hang around me, you'll find I'm actually quite boring. So, what I'm about to describe to you isn't something that happens every Thursday afternoon. It has only happened to me one other time in my life, and that was on June 4, 1994. It's so uncommon that I remember the specific dates.

The encounter started when I heard an audible voice while I was in my den, and I knew Who it was. The first thing He said was, "Put your computer down." Then He told me what He was about to do in my life. I didn't cry. I didn't shake. I didn't fall down. I didn't yell. I simply said, "Why?" I'm not going into all that He shared with me about my assignment. It simply is not wise to talk about everything He shares with you. I probably will at the end of my life, if I stay clean and pure and watch everything He shared that morning come to pass. But in that moment, I just said, "Why?" And He said...nothing. However, a tangible love came over me. Have you ever started crying because you just know you're accepted by God? Sometimes it happens in worship. You know everything's going to be okay. It's the moment in which you're not suicidal, but you wish you could just get sucked up into a vortex and go to heaven. By the way, if we don't get homesick for heaven from time to time we are probably are not walking with Him—we are mostly just believing in Him. We have a place at the Table but you're living in Lo-debar. For two and a half weeks, I was in what some call "the thin place." It doesn't happen all the time with me. But, for those two and a half weeks, I could not stop thinking about Him and He didn't stop talking to me. He showed me my future, He showed me my assignment, He showed me what to do. And...He tested me. I was having an awesome dramatic God encounter and I had no idea what was about to happen.

KNUCKLEBALLS

And a voice came from heaven: "You are my Son, whom I love; with you I am well pleased" (Mark 1:11-12).

It was a year and a half after that dramatic encounter in my den before I realized that what I am about to share with you did not come from the enemy, it came from our loving Father. He intentionally did something in my life that I thought was the work of the enemy. He wanted to expose a lot of Lo-debar in me. I didn't see it coming, and I was the pastor of a church. It is humbling to be following God hard and then get thrown a knuckleball when you're used to hitting softballs. If I lob you a soft ball, you can probably hit it; but if I throw you a Tim Wakefield knuckleball, you'll probably jump out of the way and get Strike One. The ball will move all over the place. When that happens spiritually, it can make you wonder what is going on. You may just want to jump out of the way. God had to throw a knuckleball at me to get me to see that I was using the language of the King's Table but there was something hidden in my own heart, and that "thing" was 100 percent orphan thinking. It wasn't a small thing either. It was a big thing.

God threw His best Tim Wakefield knuckleball at me and then He said, "Chad, I love you enough to tell you I cannot do *through* you, what I have not first done *in* you. Quit praying for the devil to get off your back. I'm going to prune you so hard because I have to get Lo-debar out of you and show you that you *talk* about the King's Table more than you *live* at it." God was about to tell me that I was walking in offense and that it was time to prune it off. I knew I used to walk in it, but I thought it was killed in me. Dead and gone. It wasn't. For two and half weeks after my big encounter in the den, I was in a thin place and it was amazing. I could have lived there for the rest of my life. I was clear about my assignment; I had zero doubts. Then one by one the Father started leading people out of my life; people that I was very close to and did life with. Seven guys that I did life with on a weekly basis left the church in which I pastor. We very rarely saw each other much after that. When I watched them walk away, something I didn't even know existed bubbled up from my heart. Then I did what most of us do, especially guys. I kept my John Wayne face on and pushed that thing right back down where it came from. Trouble is, that doesn't work long-term. When something is bubbling in your heart, it's not a matter of whether it's bubbling, it's a matter of whether you will deal with what's being exposed. You see, spiritual orphans think that God exposes things to punish us and condemn us. But that's not true. It is pure grace and pure love that motivates Him to expose these things in us. When my friends left our church, I started picking up on vibes from the Father that said, "You need to prepare for some bumpy waters, and it doesn't have anything to do with anyone else in your life. The bumpy waters concern your heart. This isn't about your wife, and it isn't about your kids. This isn't about your assignment or your friends. Chad, I love you enough to tell you that you have such a big blind spot in you that, if I don't help you and if I don't heal you of this, you will never be able to fulfill your assignment."

What does offense look like? I don't think anyone would ever admit to every bit of this language; but here are some thoughts we all have, even though we might not say them out loud:

> *You hurt my feelings.*
>
> *I feel betrayed.*
>
> *I'm going to harbor unforgiveness for a long time.*
>
> *I can't stand even the thought of you.*
>
> *I will judge you, condemn you, avoid you, and even slander you.*
>
> *How dare you hurt me, you will never hurt me again.*
>
> *I am disappointed in you. You did not meet my expectations.*

While some of those sound ridiculous to say out loud, there are probably a few that hit really close to home. When my friends left our church, my offended heart didn't match the way I was speaking with my mouth. My offense manifested with me being silent, internalizing the pain, and thinking it was all about me. I felt abandoned. How could they leave me? I will never forget the day the Father said, "Chad, you've never been the point of your own narrative." Isn't it interesting how God can say difficult things to us and yet we sense His tenderness as He relays what's on His mind?

So, there I was—using Table language but living like a spiritual orphan off and on. I did not want to stay there, so I started making my way back to the King's Table. I started growing in friendship with the Father. Then He said, "Chad, there is one more deathblow I need to give to you. Luke 9:23 is going to be both your best friend and your worst friend for a while, because you think it has started, but it hasn't started yet." At times like these you can be tempted to lean back into Lo-debar because you're actually seeking the approval of those closest to you more than you are seeking obedience to God's approval. When God said that to me...well, you can't exactly say, "Get behind me, satan" when you hear things like that from God. I knew it was Him—His sheep hear His voice.

STARVING UNTO DEATH

When you squeeze a lemon, lemon juice comes out. When Father squeezes a Christian, often offense comes out. I want the Father to squeeze me and I want Jesus to come out. There was only one way He could get me to the place where He could squeeze me and Jesus would come out more. He didn't accomplish this by telling me how great I was. He did it by taking me into a desert and starving me of the things I thought I needed. He started to open up my eyes by asking, "Why do you act a different way around certain people? Why do you strive for the approval of so many people?" I said, "Just kill me, just kill me." The deathblow was coming. Have you ever gone through a season where the Father is quiet on purpose, because He is starving something in you?

Then I was given another a strong prophetic word from a prophet who lives out of state. I didn't know whether I wanted to fight him or run from him. He said, "God's been chipping away at you, but this last thing is the deathblow. If you will open yourself up, He wants to kill this thing before anything happens in your life." When He said that, I almost didn't want to receive it. But I needed to. The truth is, if you are in a deep level of Lo-debar, sometimes the best thing Father can do is to not caress you out of it. Sometimes the best thing Father can do is to starve you of whatever's in you that is not supposed to be there. It isn't about making you feel terrible about yourself. The whole purpose of what you are going through is to be groomed into the image of Jesus Christ. It is not your platform. It is not your gift. It is not your family. It is not your destiny. It is this simple question, "Are you growing in the image of Jesus, the most selfless human to ever live?" Until I get to a place of selflessness, I can believe in Him, but I'm not one with Him. Let's get real, we're all selfish. We all get offended. I am growing. I am allowing Him to show me my blind spots, even when it hurts. I want my heart to be like His. I want to love others like He does. The only one who can change is me. It all started with that simple prayer—"Search my heart." For me, the best thing that could have happened to me was to have the people that I was very close to leave and not be in my life anymore on a regular basis. What I thought was the enemy stirring up conflict in my life was a loving Father's pleasure to groom me for something He wanted to do through me. I am a firm believer that God will remove any crutch in our lives that takes the place of only what He wants to fulfill. The need for approval from others was something that was driving my life and I did not even know it.

If we run towards our destinies without having the character of Jesus, it can end up disastrous. If God puts His hand on

The Garden Greenville and it helps many people, but I have an obsession with approval, I'll be done within one to two years. Approval, appetite and ambition are never satisfied. You have to continually feed them to feel content. Even though my blind spot had to do with approval, the same principles apply for any stumbling block. If you are man enough or woman enough, if you are tired of feeding your own needs, then do something. Just ask the Father what's inside of you that needs to be exposed and let Him deal with it; let Him be the gardener; don't tell Him how to prune you. I have never seen a crepe myrtle say, "Hey take it easy, Hoss." The crepe myrtle just needs to say, "Oh boy," and know that if the Father wants to prune it so low that it looks like a stump, then He's only doing it because He deems it worthy of explosive growth. The same is true when the Father prunes us. Growth only comes through death. Hear me out: your spouse is not your problem. Your boss is not your problem. Your friends are not the problem. Many times, the enemy is not your problem. You know who the problem is? The guy or gal in the mirror. When the Father starts pruning, here is what orphans say: "Well, I knew it. You hate me; that's why You're pruning me. You hate me. You're only pointing out bad things to me." I was in that place. But God, through tears, was saying to me, "Chad, if you will just let Me do this, you have no idea of the fruit you'll bear. If you will just let me do this you will get to enjoy the fruit. You must allow me to take the blade to the root if you want to enjoy the fruit." This is how it works in the Kingdom. You have fruit that is growing until the day He comes to prune you. Pruning does not just happen once in your lifetime, or in only one area of your life. As you permit Him to prune you, to remove your own selfishness. Then, over seasons of pruning and growth, you will grow into a mighty oak tree. Remember the mighty oaks of righteousness planted by streams of living water. When you've grown into a mighty oak, people can come and take shade under your obedience to Him.

Everyone wants the identity and the promise that He is going to use us to do great things, yet few want to submit to the Father's pruning process. Very few really want God to squeeze them to see what comes out. It's the spiritual sons and spiritual daughters who just say, "You can have all of me. You can have all of me." They are the ones who bear fruit.

TRUSTING HIM

Things change when you give up offense. One of those spiritual sons who left called me. He had no idea I was writing about offense. We met at a restaurant, sat down, and he said, "I owe you." I told him that he owed me nothing. As a matter of fact, I owed him a "thank you." I told him that I owed all of them who left, a thank you. Later, as I got to thinking of those whose approval I had been seeking, I was reminded of everything God has been doing within me. I now realize that at the time of the exodus from The Garden Greenville, I just didn't know or understand what God was doing. When you can't understand what He's doing, it's okay; just be patient. Trust Him beyond your own understanding.

If I plant potatoes and go out the next day and start screaming at them to grow, God is going to have to tell me that my method won't work. There's a thing called seedtime harvest.

Wouldn't it be great if God just said, "Okay, I'm going to get all the Lo-debar out of you just by blowing on you, and just like that it will be done?" That's not how He does things. Realistically, it may take you two years to get rid of all your orphanhood thinking. You can't get there today, but you can start today by taking responsibility for yourself. Begin by saying, "God, I'm done with this. And while you're at it—while you're killing the approval thing, you might as well just kill the appetite thing, and kill the ambition thing too. Just kill it all. Kill it all." When you can do this, you can get to the end yourself and you can start to sound like Paul. You learn to be content in all things. You're no longer focused on the fruit. Someone can give you a compliment and you don't even feel it; you don't even hear it because you no longer need it. I am living proof of this. When I was a high-level orphan, I'd get offended if you just looked at me wrong. Now, sometimes I get compliments and I hardly even hear them. When we allow God to prune, transformation follows.

Only God can transform us. We can't transform ourselves. We can open ourselves and ask Him to search us and kill everything He doesn't want within us. Yet, we can't transform ourselves. The only thing that can help us is death at the cross, picking up our own cross, and following Him. When we do that, our stuff just starts falling off us. Paul was struck blind, went into the Arabian desert for three years and Jesus just pecked away at him. God said, "Paul, I am going to show you how much you must suffer for me." Paul was in a jail cell, about to be killed, but he wasn't drowning in offense. Instead, he was reflecting on just how good the Lord is. There's proof—you can get to the end of yourself. It is possible. It's a great day when you come to the end of yourself and you know that offense is being killed in you. When you're around people who used to offend you—perhaps it's even your ex-spouse—and you've got nothing but love and blessing for them, you'll know offense is being killed. The death of offense is a monumental thing.

FROM CONFLICT TO CHARACTER

I used to think that all conflict came from the enemy. Now, I think a lot of conflict is caused by the Father and we just think it's the enemy. Only in conflict do you truly find out who you really are. Conflict will also reveal the character of those around you. Without tension you do not have friends, you have acquaintances. Without conflict, you do not have a true family. Conflict transforms us. Conflict forces you to see what is in you that can be transformed into the image of Christ, who was the perfect representation of Father. As you are transformed, you find that you hold on to less. You can choose to be your own master, or owner, holding onto every offense and holding onto unforgiveness, or you can choose to let Him be the Master. When He is the Master, I can let Him groom me to forgive. I can let Him groom me to release offense. I release the need to be right. When that happens, I can have nothing but love for whoever I was in conflict with. The highest level of sonship is, *"Abba, forgive them for they do not know what they are doing."*

People say to me often that they want community, but the truth is that we cannot have community if we are not willing to have conflict. The flip side is you really cannot grow without community. It is not just you and Jesus alone. It is you and

Jesus and the rest of the family. If the goal is selflessness, the path to that selflessness runs through conflict, not peace. When I go through conflict, it makes me lean into the Father more. Perhaps what you're going through with your boss right now isn't from the enemy. What if the Father is grooming you through someone who doesn't even know Him? What would His purpose be in doing this? To groom you into the image of Jesus. He's not trying to groom you into the image of an author. He's not trying to groom you into the image of a leader. He's actually trying to groom you into the image of a follower of His Son. Everyone wants to lead; few want to follow. Let's say your life falls apart, but your character is growing in Jesus Christ. It seems like nothing is being blessed around you. However, He's telling you, "You're one of My closest friends." Do you care more about the abundance you feel is missing or the friendship you have with Him?

Paul's answer to that question is obvious from his life and writings. Paul went to Malta, healed everyone on the island, and shortly thereafter, when he knew it was the end of his life, he wrote in Philippians: "I just want to know You. I just want to know You, and the power of Your resurrection. I just want to know You" (see Phil. 3). He was saying all that as he was about to die.

If we're not careful, we will use the language of the King's Table and seem prosperous while we're actually living in Lo-de-bar. Back in the 1960s, cocaine was the addiction of choice. Now, in the 21st century, the addiction of choice is the "like" button on social media. We're addicted. We live our lives through the like button. What if God did something great through you and you said, "You know what, instead of telling the world how great I am right now, I'm just going to take a break?" This is not meant as condemnation. I'm just sharing my story, my journey. I've gone from lying in a fetal position on the kitchen floor to accepting this truth about life as a spiritual son at the King's Table. I wish I could tell you that the journey from Lo-debar to the King's Table is quick and easy, but I can't. Maybe the goal is to just keep coming to the Table. Don't stop coming to the Table. When you drop the ball and realize you've walked in a low level of offense for two years, don't beat yourself up. Instead, just say to the Father, "Why do I still have Lo-debar in me?" He wants you to keep coming to the Table. If you stay in Lo-debar, then you're defined by your depression, by your offense, by your anger. You are defined by words that are contrary to His Word, and to the culture of the Kingdom and the family Table. You do not have to stay in Lo-debar. Just get up, like the lame man after 38 years, and say, "I can't do this anymore." When depression rears its head at you, when excuse rear its head, just say, "Enough! I declare war!" Then, put yourself in community and be big enough to ask those around you to speak into your life. Refuse to hide. Just keep coming to the Table. The invitation of this entire book is to let go of Lo-debar and come to the King's Table, leaving offense behind in the dust. No matter how difficult it seems, never stop coming to the Table. When the ideology of remaining at the Table becomes the norm for your life, you will see fruit; you will see your gifts grow.

CHAPTER FIFTEEN

LIVING AS GOD'S ORIGINAL

God loves an original. The more we get connected to Him, the more free we are to simply be ourselves and enjoy Him and the fact that He made us and is very comfortable with us being an original. I took my kids to the zoo recently and this point was made clear when I was standing there staring at the baboons. I'm not sure there is a more awkward looking animal in the world. The whole time I'm standing there looking at their flared red back side, I'm thinking, "Father, you made them." I'm sure at one point there was a thought of, "How about we put a monkey on the earth that looks awkward. How about we flare the butt and make it red just to keep things original and fun." Whether we like it or not, God has a sense of humor. Perhaps we get our humor from the Father Himself, since we are made in His image and likeness. As I stood there at the zoo that day I was keenly aware that the Father loves originals. I literally can't imagine what it must have been like for Noah to watch all of those animals board that boat. There were so many types of animals that God created. There are so many types of plants, trees, and flowers that came from the creative heart of God. Yet so many people who struggle to stay at the King's Table of intimacy with God find it almost impossible to believe that we are all original in God's eyes.

Recently I was ministering at a friend's church when the Father showed me a picture of how He values Kentucky Fried Chicken over Bojangles.' Now, I totally get that some people reading this will not take me seriously because God would "never say anything like this." Well, He showed me a picture indicating that He values the original over a copycat every single time. Why would He use Kentucky Fried Chicken? Because KFC prides itself for being the original fried chicken fast food restaurant. There have been many to emulate them over the years, like Bojangles', but the one thing that KFC can say is that they were the original fast food restaurant to sell fried chicken. God doesn't intend that we live as spiritual orphans, finding our identity in someone other than God Himself. We are each an original and He wants us to live like we know it.

The journey to our identity looks different for each of us. It is largely up to us. We start by getting into a place where we are not placing blame on anyone or anything for our lack of relationship with God. There needs to come a point where we simply say, "I can't live in Lo-debar anymore. I must pick up my mat and walk toward friendship with Him." We need to con-secrate our self to God. The Hebrew word for *consecration* is *Qadash,* which sounds a bit like something you put on a high-end taco in Manhattan. It means "consecrate, set apart, dedi-cate." *Qadash* assumes personal responsibility and is driven by hunger. Hunger is about consecration. It is personal. No one can eat for me. Imagine going to a feast and saying, "No thank you, I will just be satisfied watching everyone else enjoy their food." Consecration is more than just looking religious, it is a personal decision to go through the season of pruning, discipline and sacrifice. It is laying down your own agenda for His. One of our greatest challenges is to get our identity from Elohim Himself. Father, Son, and Holy Spirit is where we find our greatest nourishment. When you get to the point of understanding your identity, and accepting the uniqueness of how He created you, and stop comparing yourself to others, you realize that you have reached a whole new level of consecration.

In Matthew 11:30 the Lord said that His yoke is easy and His burden is light. If the Lord's yoke is easy and His burden is light, then when I'm around you, I should feel lighter and more refreshed. So many Christ followers that I grew up with made me feel heavy and burdened. Because of this I literally associated God with a dreadful and heavy burden. I am convinced that a heavy, burdened heart is a roadblock to building deep friendship with God. For so long, I thought God hated me and that He killed my granddad. I thought He was the reason for my depression and anxiety. I had to allow God to rewire my brain because my thought patterns were so confused. Jesus loved to step into chaos and bring shalom and peace. The question that I want to be asking myself on a regular basis is, "Do I step into chaos and bring peace or is it the opposite?"

One of the fun realities of walking in deep friendship with God is that we begin to display His personality through our personality. I want people to think of me as someone who carries love, joy, peace, patience, kindness, goodness, faithfulness, gentleness, and self-control. Instead of beating ourselves up for what we lack in these areas, we need to simply ask Holy Spirit to show us how to make the journey from Lo-debar to the King's Table, to that place where we can enjoy intimacy with the Father, Jesus, and Holy Spirit, and share in their characteristics. We should constantly be asking ourselves if we are moving towards the King's Table and who are we bringing with us.

I believe with all of my heart that seriousness is not a fruit of the spirit. In fact, God has shown me that this is a key to walking in a deep level of the prophetic. There have been people leave The Garden Greenville because they are so serious about seriousness that anything else is offensive. As for me, I care more about understanding His character and nature than anything in the world. When I heard Him tell me that I would learn to cook, I shook my head. It blows my mind that as huge as He is, He also has a side to Him that simply wants to talk to me about cooking. As a result of this encounter, I've gotten into the habit of asking for His help when I go to the grocery store because I now know He's into the little things of my life like cooking. I want to talk to God so much that I hear Him on even the mundane things in life. If we are not careful, we will make God more spiritual than He really is and not realize that the same God that walked with Adam in the cool of the day is the same God that likes to walk with us in the everydayness of our lives.

The thing I love about building deep friendship with God is that we are always learning what He is like. We can't get to the end of Him. Just when you think you are so close to Him and understand how He is wired, He goes and says something that jars you. I was jarred when I heard Him talk to me about cooking in heaven. He knows what makes me happy and He spoke into my heart that day. Biblically speaking, this kind of response from God makes perfect sense. In gospel of Luke, there are three parables involving different people—a joyful woman, a joyful servant, and a joyful father. Do you see a pattern? We will enter into His presence with joy and lots of celebration. I have come to find the Father, Jesus, and Holy Spirit to be the three most joyful persons I have ever met. God's personality is full of absolute joy and celebration. The part of this that should make us nervous is the reality that so many of His children on the earth don't seem to carry a lot of joy.

I've done the religious, depressed, miserable thing and now a lot of people call me strange because I have a high value for joy and celebration. I have noticed over the last fifteen years of walking with the Holy Spirit that some people that I am around seem to have a difficult time "respecting" my leadership because there seems to be a presupposition that in order to lead on a high level in His Kingdom, we need to be very serious people. Lightheartedness and childlike simplicity, joy, and celebration seem to be associated more with kids than adult leaders. Maybe we have the whole thing wrong. The other day a friend of mine was over at our house eating breakfast with my family. I had an impression from God to serve my friend's food on our red celebration plate for birthdays. When I put the plate on the table, my friend said, "How did you know it was my birthday?" The truth is that I did not know it was his birthday, but God did, and this small gesture from God through me touched his heart. Perhaps God is more lighthearted than we think. Perhaps He highly values celebration. Perhaps many of us are more serious than God is. Perhaps we have a distorted view of what seriousness should look like in the Kingdom of God.

I was praying over someone recently and God gave me a date. It happened to be this person's birthday. In moments like this, people are literally blown away that God cares about the whole world and also us as individuals. I have seen it happen time and time again—when I am giving words of knowledge over people and they break in an instant with joyful tears at the realization that the God who created all things loves to celebrate with us and the journey we are on with Him. So many of His kids fail to see that He sees us as clean as Jesus and relates to us with a critical eye but not a critical spirit. I think we need to be really careful who we allow to speak into our lives on a continual basis. For example, why would I allow someone who has no fruit or joy in their life to teach me the ways of the Kingdom of God? We tend to value the intellect or influence of very serious people, and gravitate towards them, while ignoring the fact that there is very little if any proof of the fruit of joy and celebration in their lives. One of the things that I look for in people as evidence of the fruit of friendship with God is how they celebrate. We should be very nervous to open ourselves up for someone to influence us that does not value what God values.

I think we tend to assume that someone who walks in joy and celebration is just wired a certain way in his or her personality. I believe it has more to do with simply being connected to

God in a deep way. It is absolutely impossible to be great friends with God and not carry these attributes. My life changed when I realized how much Jesus walked in these attributes during His life on the earth. When God gave me revelation that Jesus put a face on the Father, I became so excited to know that God is a person of joy and celebration. I have never in my life understood how someone can be a disciple, be leading in the Kingdom, and not carry joy and celebration on an ongoing basis. In so many ways, Jesus completely offended the religious culture of His day with these two attributes. He openly displayed a passion for joy and celebration. It is incredible to realize that even His first miracle of turning water into wine is a picture of these two values.

The Pharisees had large portions of the Scriptures memorized and yet got offended with how joyful Jesus was. Such things were looked down upon. Yet, along came their covenant-cutting God and said, "My first miracle will be wine at a celebration wedding." His opening act of the miraculous in the New Testament was making wine manifest. It was a lot of wine and was found to be absolutely delicious. If we are not careful, we will not be too much different from the Pharisees while ignoring the fact that Jesus is the same yesterday today and forever. Celebration is not something that He used to value. It is part and parcel of who He actually is. He is the God of celebration.

I love to ask God a lot of questions. I asked Him the one day, "What am I going to do when I first get to heaven?" He replied, "Chad, you are going to have the biggest feast you have ever had in your life. You will also learn how to cook. You've always wanted to be a fantastic cook." I'm sure that His answer will make many eyes roll because it's not serious enough for many people who follow God. I can't say that this is what I was expecting Him to say. If you would have asked me what His answer would have been, I probably would have leaned more in the direction of, "You will learn to worship me forever and continue to grow in revelation of my greatness throughout all time." Although I'm sure that those two things will happen when I'm up there, that is not what He told me. I think some of us are too serious and tightly wound to hear God on an ongoing basis. Some of us associate God with nothing but a heaviness and seriousness, perhaps forgetting that He is also our Father. If the Lord Jesus' yoke is easy and His burden is light, then that is the way in which the Father is wired as well.

More than anything, I desire to see God move all over the world in power. I want Him to start with me. It has to be possible to see naturally supernatural cultures established everywhere by His sons and daughters who are abiding and feasting at the King's Table. It happened in the book of Acts. It's been happening since then in pockets of places where people experience the things that the Father is so passionate about. He still loves to heal and deliver. He still loves to use common people to do extraordinary things in His Kingdom. He still desires family and deep friendship with His sons and daughters.

I sincerely pray that you will take a step out of the boat toward the invitation to walk away from spiritual orphanhood in Lo-debar and take your seat at the King's Table as a spiritual son or daughter. I pray you will also accept the invitation to live a supernatural life—a life where your common church starts seeing uncommon breakthrough because you are willing to lead in courageous ways. I pray that you decide to become passionate about the things that Jesus was so passionate about in His ministry. Other people's breakthrough hinges on our desire to be courageous and lead out in the way in which Jesus would lead out if He were on the earth leading our churches. He was passionate about God's family then and He is now. He was passionate about re-connecting us to Eden, about inviting us to the King's Table then, and He is now. He was passionate about the supernatural then, and He is now.

Come, Lord Jesus. Help us.

EPILOGUE

Over the last 20 years, I have been surprised to see how many people God has helped know Him better as the result of me sharing my story of brokenness. I think many of us look up to people who stand on stage and are great speakers. We flock to conferences hoping to receive from these great leaders and communicators. In an era that has been defined by popularity when it comes to many ministers, we are now starting to see that perhaps we don't need as many high-profile leaders to help us get to know God on a deeper level as we maybe once thought. If I've learned anything over my career, it's been that I typically find God in places that I did not go looking for Him. I found Him in my own mess and I continue to find Him as I tell others about what God did for me in my mess.

I think that God is found more in the messes of life than most of us believe. Over my life, I have bonded with Him deeply when life has hurt. What I did not know then that I know now is that God's recipe for us to walk in a high level of power is to actually be open and vulnerable about our own brokenness. My wife and I say often that we don't trust people that don't walk with a limp. What we mean by this is that it's easier to trust someone who has gone through something deeply humbling and has seen God bring them through it. I highly encourage you to be open about the possibility of not only inviting God into your mess but also inviting Him into showing you how you can share the testimony of your mess and God's faithfulness.

Paul boasted in his weaknesses and saw a power come through his life that he could not have gotten without boasting in those weaknesses. Grace flows to the lowest places and when you become vulnerable about how you are incapable of any victory outside of the help of God, you will see God show up.

Saul of Tarsus was not looking for God when he had that "Road to Damascus" experience. I have read the story of many addicts that were not looking for God on their worst night of addiction, but they ended up encountering Him. Many people find God in their journey through cancer and other life-threatening sicknesses. What if what you have experienced in your mess is actually someone else's recipe for their own victory? Perhaps it's time to start telling your story. You simply never know what God can do with your own courage as you give Him your mess. He has an unusual way of making our messes our message if we will be courageous enough to tell our narratives. Take a chance on that and see what He will do.

ABOUT CHAD NORRIS

Chad Norris is the senior pastor of Bridgeway Church in Greenville, SC. He has a master of divinity from Beeson Divinity School and is currently working toward a doctorate at Regent University. Chad and his wife, Wendy, have three children and are passionate to create a culture of discipleship that begins in their own home and extends to everything they do.

YOUR
Prophetic
COMMUNITY

Are you passionate about hearing God's voice, walking with Jesus, and experiencing the power of the Holy Spirit?

Destiny Image is a community of believers with a passion for equipping and encouraging you to live the prophetic, supernatural life you were created for!

We offer a fresh helping of practical articles, dynamic podcasts, and powerful videos from respected, Spirit-empowered, Christian leaders to fuel the holy fire within you.

Sign up now to get awesome content delivered to your inbox
destinyimage.com/sign-up

 Destiny Image